On Turtles and Dragons
and the dangerous quest for a media art notation system

ed. Version 1.2

© Tim Boykett, Marta Peirano, Simone Boria, Heather Kelley, Elisabeth Schimana, Andreas Dekrout, Robert Rotenberg 2012-2013.

A catalogue record for this book is available from the British Library.

ISBN: 978-1-300-94360-0

Times Up Press
Industriezeile 33b
4020 Linz
Austria

Website: www.timesup.org
E-mail address: info@timesup.org
Phone: +43 732 - 787804

Book Sprint facilitation by: Adam Hyde
Website: www.booksprints.net
E-mail address: adam@booksprints.net

Cover Design: Marta Peirano/Johannes Grenzfurthner/Tina Auer

This book was produced using Booktype and BookJS from Sourcefabric.

CONTENTS

FOREWORD   1

1. On Turtles and Dragons   3

2. Notes from the Sprint   5

3. What are we talking about?   7

THOUGHTS ON NOTATION   13

4. A General Catalogue of Notation Systems   15

5. Purposes for Notation   27

6. The Agency of the Map   41

7. Turtles all the way down   49

8. Beethoven's Deathbed   59

9. Steal This Notation!   65

10. It's the Cultural Context, Schtoopid!   75

INTERACTIVITY   77

11. What is Interactivity?   79

12. Slug n°. 1: Notating the Rubik's Cube   89

13. Slug n°. 2: Pong   95

A FEW SPECIMENS   105

14. Introduction to the Examples   107

15. Hacking Choreography series (2012)   109

16. Black Box Sessions (2008)   115

17. Sitting in My Chair (2001)   119

18. Formocracy (2012)   125

19. We Tell Stories (2008)   131

20. Gestural Notation   135

21. Isorhythmic Variations (2006)   139

22. The Great Score (2001 to 2006)   141

23. 20 Seconds into the Future (2010)   145

SOME WORDS TO FINISH WITH   149

24. References   151

25. A Closing Cake   153

Foreword

ON TURTLES AND DRAGONS

Welcome to the record of our mission. We set off, brave knights in somewhat polished armour upon steeds fleet of foot, out to survey the lands of the realm and come back with interesting stories, with special interests in a few less explored regions off in one corner of the lands.

We liken our foray to the construction of a map. As you know, at the edges of a map where none fear to tread, we believe there be dangers and things of which we cannot speak, and therefore prefer to remain silent. As we approach such areas of investigation, we realise that our discussions have the habit of becoming self referential and complex, or begin to recognize that we paltry few are no match for the matters of concern. Dragons appear on a map where nothing can be found.

And thus we will speak of dragons as those areas from which we retreated, fearful of getting lost or losing too much time and being distracted from our main area of interest.

It has been five days of Book Sprint. Six invitees came together in order to map out some parts of the territory of interest. We have found several phrases for what interests us and seem to find the problematic areas of notation for interactive systems to be suitably general.

And so it was that we came together armed only with a handful of ideas each and fingers ready to type. As Paul Erdős liked to say, our "brains are open!" and they certainly were. The five days were a continual cycle of discussion, collection, sorting, writing, revising and back to it.

It was good to have help because the investigation deep into the forest of interactivity turned out to be harder and more plagued with difficulties than we ever could have imagined. An investigation of interactivity and ways to notate it was our goal, so the later chapters reflect our investigations and attempts to communicate to one another the ideas and problems with which we worked and fought to look at the problems of notating interactivity.

A phenomenon encountered early on in the discussion of notation is the "bottomless stack of turtles" effect: the infinite regress of information layers, all of which could be expressed through some kind of notation. Peel off one successfully notated strata and beneath it lies another, and beyond that still another. Yet not all these levels of focus are equally useful for the expression, discussion, or transmission of a particular piece of work to a specific audience. In contrast to dragons, these reptiles are friendly and slow and immensely patient. As we outline below, we came to see the stack of turtles, a metaphor for recursion and layering, as a way of navigating the complex hierarchies of notational

Foreword

techniques and points of view. For us the turtle has become a symbol of sympathy and subjectivity, the walls are anointed with cartoons of them and our imaginations are filled with turtles as ways of thinking things.

This book is a manifestation of what happened over these days. We hope it is of interest, that the things we saw and the conversation we had will be relevant to more than a few other souls, whether they be practitioners or researchers, notaters, diagrammaticists or analysers. Note that the writing group is varied and our voices are mixed - you, the reader, will find changes and modulations in tone, perhaps the odd disagreement even. Please do not let them put you off. Feel free to join us. For we hope that some other brave knights will mount their steeds and, perhaps armed better to conquer certain dragons, further illuminate some corners of the realm. The map will lose some of its white patches and give up some of its secrets. And reveal a few more dragons themselves.

NOTES FROM THE SPRINT

This is an idiosyncratic book. Written in five days by six people, it not only displays but also relishes the unevenness that this process creates. While several post sprint workovers have removed some sharp corners and made the general experience less tumultuous, these distinct voices remain present.

So as you read this, indulge yourself in the fantasy of listening in to a longer symposium, a discussion between several people who came together to think, discuss, argue, dissect and write about their understandings of notation. Multiple points of view, mother tongues and fields of interest are present and presented here. From legal experts, composers, programmers, radio and print journalists, anthropologists, game designers, knotters, knitters and mathematicians come so many mutually incompatible ideas that there can be no single common voice. Each of us managed to confuse, excite and bamboozle the other with reinterpretations of one another's areas of expertise. Some of the reinterpretations made it into this book, we hope that they are of value. Others have been left gasping in the sprint while a few remain half written in the earlier version of the writing space.

As you read, you will encounter some ideas that are familiar and others that are new. Feel free to jump around in the text. There are repetitions as various contributors define and explain ideas in slightly different ways.

Some homogenisation has been carried out. We hope that a consistent form of typography has been introduced. All references are collected in a chapter at the back of the book. There are still some that have been omitted, but in the age of instantaneous google-isation, we presume that you will find the referenced works.

The version you are reading is at least the fourth. Perhaps there have been further reviews since then. We welcome input, active as well as passive. Suggestions of examples are as valuable as whole new chapters. Spelling corrections, image refinement and better referencing are all welcome. While we do not pretend that this is an academic text, there are several academics among the writers, as well as practitioners and both of these types are people who like to hear suggestions about what could be taken further, developed or refined. We would enjoy the inclusion of some of the less worked out ideas into future versions, by people who are able to contemplate those ideas in an interesting fashion. Be welcomed.

But now, into the fray.

Foreword

WHAT ARE WE TALKING ABOUT?

"Everything is brown"[1]
".... ‾ . .‾. ‾.‾‾ ‾ ..... .‾. ‾‾. .. ... ‾.... .‾. ‾‾‾ .‾‾ .‾ ‾. "

As with so many things, it is best to start where we feel most comfortable. And that might as well be breakfast.

> *"Take 2 chicken eggs per person and break them into a bowl. Heat a pan to medium temperature. Add salt, pepper, and one teaspoon of milk per egg to the bowl. Mix for 2 minutes. Put one teaspoon of butter per egg into the heated pan. Add the mixture from the bowl. When the mixture starts to solidify scrape and mix with wooden spoon until all of the mixture is firm. Serve with toast."*

Completely obvious as to what it will produce, this highly formalised language of a recipe is an easily grasped notation. It is readily apparent what will come out, but it is of interest to see how the proportions are decided. The text form describes the process quite exactly, allowing little room for error or interpretation. This might be seen as a good notation for a very concrete process.

This book arose as an attempt to collect and collate various ideas and problems around notation that many of us have been dealing with on several levels. We have processes of varying complexity, and we would like to work out ways to discuss them that move beyond the extremes of handwaving and looking at the deepest level of code. For example: How do we remember the structures of the facilitation systems that we have developed and pass them on to others? How do we discuss the possibilities for interaction, and the way a media should be playing, given the actions of possible visitors? How do we investigate the inner workings of an experience to see whether it makes sense, without building it completely in advance?

We want to think of notation as an abstraction, a simplification, an intuitive or studied way of writing something down that succinctly summarises the important points of a given situation, process, object or system.

And then we woke up.

The borders of the phenomenon of "notation" behave like Tantalos' fruit, hanging just in reach until we attempt to reach for them. As soon as a limiting feature seems to be within reach, an example or sometimes an argument will betray that limiting power from the just discovered feature, and lift those borders to the sky. For the purpose of meaningful

Foreword

exchange on the subject of the phenomenon of "notation", a common terminology is as indispensable as a discretionary border to the field of discussion. We do not want to bite off more than we can chew.

Some Definitions of a Sort

The set of attributes used here is put together for practical reasons only. It is not chosen completely arbitrarily but in search of a "lowest common denominator" which may appear incorrect or unjustified in some (we hope rare) cases. Some dragons will have to be slain at another time.

For the sake of clarity in expression, "notation" will, unless specifically stated otherwise (or obvious from the context), be used to refer to a concrete example, a concrete use of a notation system. A "notation system" consists of all the possible forms of representation, rules and dependencies that make sense within that system. Within a given notation system, all possible forms of representation will be referred to as the "vocabulary" of that system. The sum of all rules and relations within a notation system will be called the system's "inner logic".[2]

Many names exist for a given piece of notation in the respective notational system. A recipe, a score, some pseudocode, a script. New possibilities require that we extend a piece of notation. When the microwave oven arrived, the terminology for its use had to be created, and before then the electric beater. As recipes are written in a slightly formalised way using natural language, such additions were easy to make, and the notational system of recipes became a little larger and more complex. When tape players as a new musical instrument or extended playing techniques were added to concert music performances, an extension of musical notation of staves had to be found.

The *semantic content* of a given piece of vocabulary is of importance. The same phrase could mean similar yet very significantly different things when imagined as dance, acoustic or mathematical notation. For instance the symbolic statement A->B, where we say "from A to B" might refer to a movement of a dancer across the stage, the change of an actor between emotional states or a mathematical function between two sets. It is vital that we agree upon such semantic contents - fundamental misunderstandings can arise if not. This is perhaps one of the critical parts in the creation of a notation system, or the decision to use a particular notation system. Constructivists never tire of claiming that meaning is negotiated, and it is by no means less true in this case. This will be seen later as we examine several examples, where the semantics of each symbol need to be explained or discussed.

3. What are we talking about?

When thinking about notation as a phenomenon of human behaviour, some examples pop up right away. Musical scores, geographical maps and mathematical diagrams might be amongst the most common and widespread forms. These and all other more or less exotic, ancient and helpful uses of notation systems all have their own inner logic, their own vocabulary of signs and symbols and their own purpose. Each notation system is arbitrary when viewed from the outside and a complete universe, a "reality" with its own rules and logic from within. Each of these discretionary human-created realities is focused on very specific aspects considered relevant and deliberately ignores or at least leaves open others.

We can look at a notation system not as an answer to a specific question but as tool to produce answers to a specific type of question or problem and to preserve, communicate, or reproduce those relevant aspects. This highlights their essence, the indispensable core attributes that a system must have to be a notation system.

A system becomes a notation system when it has a working inner logic using a set of abstract representations (vocabulary) of aspects of potentially universal experience deemed relevant to be differentiated between, preserved or communicated about.

This definition includes all communication, all language, and especially (here be dragons!) all forms of written language. So the only reasonable thing to do is to add restrictions to the list of notation system attributes: the purpose of communicating *about* something specific while intentionally *not* communicating about something else. This leaves out communication *per se* (as an end in itself) as too general to be usefully discussed here. The restrictive prerequisite of being externalised - of a system existing independently from the person who uses it - has to be seen in the same light: it keeps our subject specific enough to be useful.

The "Is it a Notation System?" Test

We sometimes found that we were speaking of things that, upon closer inspection, were not really notational systems. We refined our idea and thought that, in order to keep our heads clear, we would try to find a process to help identify the quality of something as a notation system. The following test is intended to be applied in a sequential fashion to a given system to see how well it conforms to our idea of a notational system.

Testing systems for their "notation-system-ability" (expanded below):

1. Is there an inner logic?

Foreword

    2. Is there a vocabulary?
    3. Are the notations potentially accessible to at least one entity/person?
    4. Are other aspects intentionally left out?
    5. Is it an overlooked dragon?

In detail:

1. Is there an inner logic?
   Each notation system constitutes only a section of a larger "reality" and creates its own little world made only of what is relevant from the perspective of the inner logic. Even if the described piece of reality is lacking logic, the notation system describing it doesn´t. A system to keep track of completely random and unrelated events (for instance) is consistent and logical in itself, and has structural and syntactical logic.

2. Is there a vocabulary?
   There are several criteria that come together here. Does it speak about anything? Are there things that we can notate in some way in this system? If there is nothing in the vocabulary, then there is nothing to say with it. Then the next test is whether it gets easier to talk about the area that is being notated, that is, that the system abstracts what it describes.

   A description of an object or a circumstance by the object or circumstance itself is not an abstraction. If the vocabulary notating the system is not simpler than the system being notated, then the system is not in a meaningful way a notation system, as it is not part of a focused "vocabulary system" as the description and the described are identical. Such notation systems can be found for example in hypothetical 1:1 maps where the map is of the exact size and nature as the territory. These are not only useless, but also represent the limit of the smallest possible level of abstraction (none) and the highest possible level of detail and complexity.[3]

3. Are the notations potentially accessible to at least one entity/person?[4]
   The use of a notation system which cannot be interpreted by anyone at all makes absolutely no sense. While the I-Ching sticks might reflect and thus notate my emotional state, we doubt that anyone can actually read that notation. The minimum requirement of at least one potential addressee can be seen in the example of personal short-

3. What are we talking about?

hand notes intended only for the writer herself. Usually the circle of potential "readers" is greater, and maximisation of the number of potential readers is a core motivation for the use of standardised notation systems (e.g. mathematical, musical and geographical orientation notation systems). We will look at this in more detail below in the chapter Beethoven's Deathbed.

4. Are other aspects intentionally left out?
This is very closely related to the condition of abstraction and the depth of representable level of detail. In the process of abstraction, a decision must be made on the relevance of pieces of information, deciding whether to leave them out and concentrate on others. For example, a piece of musical notation (a score) may contain instructions for the handling of a specific instrument (a pianoforte) but not the manufacturer of the instrument (Bösendorfer), the size or form of the room in which it is to be played (chamber music hall) or the individual person to play the work (Rubinstein). All these factors can and probably will influence the produced outcome, but are not considered relevant from within that specific musical notation system.

The element of intentionality is important for a reader as it is necessary to know that what was omitted was intentional, rather than being left out accidentally.

5. Is it an overlooked dragon?
Does the inclusion of a system in the notation systems under discussion have potential to increase insight into the phenomenon or practice of notation, or does it foreseeably open a door to an unanswerable argument, which at best can only lead to frustration, or worst to a metaphysical whirlpool? If the latter, it is a dragon, and we will not slay it here.

---

1. Universal "answer" to everything, perceived in the Oliver Wendell Holmes, "Mechanism in Thought and Morals," Phi Beta Kappa address, Harvard Univeristy, June 29, 1870 (Boston: J.R. Osgood and Company, 1871)
2. For those who are aware of formal language theory, the vocabulary is the set of well-formed formulas that can be formed in a given formal language, the inner logic is the syntax of the language.
3. In the sense of Kolmogorov Complexity - this thing is not

Foreword

   compressible to anything simpler than what it is.
4. Wittgenstein's Private Language Argument is considered a dragon in this context. And left to future adventurers and slayers.

Thoughts on Notation

A GENERAL CATALOGUE OF NOTATION SYSTEMS

Si (como afirma el griego en el Cratilo)
el nombre es arquetipo de la cosa
en las letras de 'rosa' está la rosa
y todo el Nilo en la palabra 'Nilo'.

If (as affirms the Greek in the Cratylus)
the name is archetype of the thing,
in the letters of "rose" is the rose,
and all the Nile flows through the word.

The Golem (Borges 1967)

Every notation system is preoccupied with the most effective ways of communicating information, so its rules and shapes depend greatly on the nature of the interpreter. The first technical question then should be: who is this notation for? Who will get it? If we attend to formal considerations, the main distinction is obvious and self-explanatory: humans and machines are very different interpreters.

Then there is the question of precision. For the human interpreter, the relationship between score and performance is directly proportional to the value of the performer or interpreter of a given notation: we are necessarily hung up on the exact proportions of a medical prescription but indulge to improvisation when following a cooking recipe. Interestingly enough, in the context of artistic performance we demand a precise execution of the score, but we dedicate our senses to everything in the performance that is not in the code.

On the other hand, extreme levels of precision in a given field can result in absurdity, as the Argentinian writer Jorge Luis Borges illustrates in his famous short story *On Exactitude in Science*. Like in the book that inspired it, Lewis Carrol's *Sylvie and Bruno Concluded*, the science of cartography becomes so ambitious that "only a map on the same scale as the empire itself will suffice", rendering the whole enterprise useless and the era of Cartography terminated.

While we can say we have produced an almost 1:1 scale map that is indeed very useful - Google's satellite photos of the earth are literal, though its use of the Mercator projection inherits its blind spot around the poles - we can handle it thanks to another kind of notation, JavaScript and XML. We see here a form of 1:1 map that has become possible through the virtualisation of information and the ease of navigation that does not require the map to be physically present to get in the way. The Era of Cartography might be terminated but the tool does not yet defy the purpose.

The following examples of notation are described here to stress the differences between the main universal systems and learn how to make the letters of "rose" into the rose, and contain every drop of the Nile between its four letters.

Gestural Notation

Apparently the beginning of everything notation-wise, *cheironomy* is the art of using hand signals to direct a musical performance. Whereas in modern conducting the notes are already specified in a written score, in cheironomy the hand signs indicate melodic curves and ornaments. Cheironomers fell out of grace when modern conducting techniques developed in the XVII century. Before Karajan, the role was fulfilled by any member of the band that happened to carry a stick; sometimes the violinist with his bow, other times a lutenist moving the neck of his instrument. Today it is mainly used as inspiration for those less metrically structured compositions which require individualized direction to specific players.

It is interesting to see what we can do with it today, maybe a funny exercise that clarifies one of the main or core purposes for using notation and notation systems: to transport information in an understandable, agreed manner, even if we only have ourselves to agree with at the end of the process. We will see this later in an example chapter. This will also come up later when talking about notation for the purpose of understanding and analysis in the next chapter. Hand and other nonverbal body signals are also well known in various subcultures including the Italian criminal cultures, where they have the expressive power akin to speech.

Scientific Notation

The scientific community is fond of notation, for very good reasons. Mathematicians, physicists, astronomers, botanists and chemists not only need to navigate impossibly huge numbers and structures but also handle slippery concepts like infinity or various species with great precision. The scientific tradition of open development requires that the abstractions innate to these practitioners' thinking patterns are kept within reach of their colleagues. Scientific developments are extended to everyone involved in the same line of research, independently of their proprietary tools or incompatible non-Roman

4. A General Catalogue of Notation Systems

Ancient Egyptian cheironomy: Wind instrument players are being guided in the music by hand signs (2563 B.C.E.)

scripts, not only because fame accrues by comprehension. Chemists have their atomic symbols and reactions and biologists their Latin sounding Linnaean taxonomy systems, allowing descriptions that ignore the difference between German *Blausäure* and the English cyanic acid, hydrogen cyanide or various other equivalent names, let alone the plethora of names of plants and animals from one language group to the next.

The scientific pursuit is very often a intermingled affair, due to the fluid communication between those subjects that used to be called Natural Science until the industrial revolution. A Venn diagram of its notation systems would reveal a high degree of promiscuity, with mathematics at the center. Quantum mechanics theory uses a kind of specific notation called Bra-ket (also known by its creator's name, the Dirac bracket) but the same notation can also be used to denote abstract vectors and linear functionals in other parts of pure and applied mathematics. Probability theory and statistics have their own conventions added to the standard mathematical notation systems, extending their applicability and abstracting what has been found to be important in the special field.

All scientific systems resolve a need for clarity, concision and reduction (though, surprisingly enough, apparently ambiguous expressions do appear even in physical and mathematical texts - there is still the cultural context). This abstract origami contains massive volumes of data in a few characters but, as it is meant to survive the evolving fashions and technologies of its time, it must be open enough, and very expandable. As a cautionary tale for those that are not, there is the ungratefully retired (and named) zenzizenzizenzic, an early notation representing the eighth power (as in the zenzizenzizenzic of 7 would be

Thoughts on Notation

the power 7^8) which, according to 16th century Welsh mathematician Robert Recorde "doeth represent the square of squares squaredly".

Such notation has now fallen away to the role of a historical oddity, and probably rightly so. The constant creation of new language within mathematics is part of its daily activity, rarely will a presentation get by without an initial definition or two. No mathematician can assume that her notation will be understood outside her area of expertise, so clear introductions are vital. Unused notation withers, as can be discovered by reading many texts over five decades old. However a standard collection of mathematical notations is passed from one generation of practitioners to the next, kept alive through constant use and refinement. Mathematicians have the advantage that because what they do must satisfy the most stringent forms of rigour, their language and thus their notation must be maximally coherent and used exactly. This means that while progress might be remarkably slow, it is completely true. Mathematicians are also very adept at ignoring their history and moving on, as there is not a series of physical intuitions that continue to serve as valid approximations. When a new mathematical idea takes hold, like group theory, then the concepts of group theory are discussed directly, without necessarily referencing the traditions of the field in the solving of polynomial equations. This ahistoricality of mathematics is a bonus and a curse.

Scientific notations are, in general, more flexible and intuitive than their mathematical counterparts. Aiming for universal applicability and simplicity, the decimal system has become more widespread than the imperial system, regardless of the fact that 12 is "more divisible" than 10, which makes it still easier to use as a daily time measurement rather than some decimal time system. The fact that 2^{10} = 1024 is almost 1000 means that we happily use the word *kilo* to mean 1024 bytes or 1000 grams and *mega* to be 2^{20} = 1,048,576 which is close enough to one million bytes. Sometimes our numerical notation systems remain as complex as Recorde's.

There are of course other disciplines that exist in the interstices of science research that do not share the exacting nature of physics or mathematics, and their ever changing notation systems reflect the elusive nature of their fields. In psychology, for example, the need for a standardized evaluation system has produced efforts like the Brief Psychiatric Rating Scale (BPRS), the Scale for the Assessment of Positive Symptoms (SAPS) or the Scale for the Assessment of Negative Symptoms (SANS) along with other measures of psychopathology, without any of them being completely satisfactory. It could be claimed

4. A General Catalogue of Notation Systems

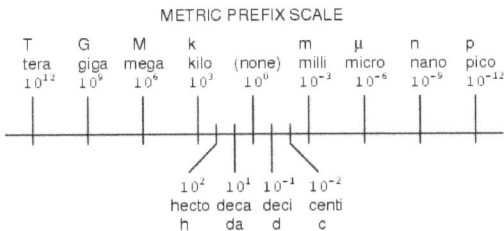

The decimal system and the derived metric system of notation has achieved widespread acceptance.

by many in the mathematical or "exact" sciences that such pieces of notational terminology are insufficiently useful to be called scientific at all. However these terms and comparisons are used and have an effective application in these disciplines, satisfying the notational requirements from the previous chapter. So let's not get too restricted in our acceptance of them.

Musical Notation

The late Canadian pianist Glenn Gould produced two masterpieces of musical genius recording the same piece with almost three decades in between. His 1955 debut recording of Bach's *Goldberg Variations* made him a legend at 22, quickly becoming one of the most famous piano recordings of all times. When the second one was released in 1981, it did so a few weeks shy of his death of a stroke at age 50. The two recordings are separated by a life of intense creative power and self-destructive addictions and couldn't be more different, both in tone and expression. In a 2002 album that includes both versions, Washington Post music critic Tim Page says "Almost anything you could say about Glenn Gould you could say the opposite and have it be somewhat true." And yet Bach's notation behind the recordings remains exactly the same.

Artistic notation is tricky, and it requires a very special kind of interpreter: an artist. This is to say, not only one with a previous specialised knowledge (just like with scientific notation, one that has learned the language) who can execute the score with the necessary precision but will also embed the performance with his own intuition, imagination, charisma, experience and insight. Those variables, that we casually call talent or even genius, cannot be notated or prescribed; they belong to the flexible and ever ambiguous field of artistic interpretation and expression. We can say that the most important part of the artistic performance is un-notateable, and any effort to notate it has been exhausted without success.

Thoughts on Notation

Faerie's Aire and Death Waltz by John Stump

That doesn't mean that such efforts haven't produced many interesting outcomes; the room for artistic expression seems to be as wide as the number of the notators dedicated to the task. An extreme example would be the infamous *Faerie's Aire and Death Waltz*, a comic score by John Stump, peppered with congenial but impossible instructions like "Release the penguins", "Remove valve" or a "Go real fast - sleepage may occurr."

More interestingly, John Cage, who famously struggled with traditional notation all his life, produced different systems for very unorthodox orchestras, sometimes with hilarious and game-changing consequences. There was *HPSCHD*, a five-hour craziness involving seven harpsichords, 52 tapes of computer-generated sounds and 64 slide projectors, and there were the *Etudes*:

> *Eleven or twelve years ago I began the Freeman Etudes for violin solo. As with the Etudes Australes for piano solo I wanted to make the music as difficult as possible so that a performance would show that the impossible is*

4. A General Catalogue of Notation Systems

not impossible and to write thirty-two of them. The notes written so far for the Etudes 17-32 show, however, that there are too many notes to play. I have for years thought they would have to be synthesized, which I did not want to do. Therefore the work remains unfinished. Early last summer ('88) Irvine Arditti played the first sixteen in fifty-six minutes and then late in November the same pieces in forty-six minutes. I asked why he played so fast. He said, "That's what you say in the preface: play as fast as possible." As a result I now know how to finish the Freeman Etudes, a work that I hope to accomplish this year or next. Where there are too many notes I will write the direction, "Play as many as possible."

Autobiographical Statement (John Cage, 1990)

Dance Notation

The most disciplined of performing arts, ballet, has produced many notation systems of its own, but the most fascinating and instructive from a technical point of view is without a doubt Vladimir Stepanov's work for the Imperial Ballet of St. Petersburg, *L'Alphabet des Mouvements du Corps Humain*. Rejecting the pictograph methodology that was the choreographic standard since the XVIII century, he chose to emulate the more precise musical score, and deconstructed every step into the most elementary movements a single part of the body can produce, encoding each movement into a "note".

The first computerized notation system, designed a century later by Eddie Dombrower for the Apple II, displayed an animated figure on the screen, following the choreographer instructions. Unsurprisingly, it didn't go very far. Today Stepanov's archives are displayed as a museum relic and his art has been replaced by a real time notation system at 1:1 scale: video recording.

Painting Notation

In the fine arts, many artistic notation systems have curiously betrayed the ambition of eliminating the artist from the art process through mechanical means, like Peter Benjamin Graham's *New Epoch Art*

21

Thoughts on Notation

An example of Vladimir Stepanov's highly abstracted dance notation.

Notation. Apparently the world's first high level visual notation system for painting, NEA "separates the act of conceiving an image from the act of painting":

> *NEA compositions are known as Sets. Sets use a unique "thematic" structure called thematic orchestration which is closely related to chaos theory in physics. This method of drawing utilizes a process apart from conventional abstraction. The raw subject matter is synthesized into a theme. A theme is a configuration of lines which embodies what the composer feels is the essence of the raw subject.*
> *The paintings are then "grown" by sensitively repeating and overlapping the themes in a rhythmic manner always with slight differences building up a complex lattice of enclosed organic and asymmetrical shapes. The theme is the "visual title" of the work. Literary titles are taken from the raw subject or from intuitive literary associations that may occur during the act of composition.*
> *Every line and every shape put where it is on purpose, no happy accidents, no random use of gesture, and no reliance on drips or splatters. Every shape asymmetrical, and unique in form; its nature and position related to every other; and its position, the overall structure, never repeating the entire evolution of the image during its making, also premeditated and in fact, containing much of its meaning; a composed image that although subject to determinism, will never repeat itself even if the entire process of making begins with identical working conditions. The child of relatively simple rules that can be applied almost effortlessly be people with reasonable sensibility and craft skill but who NEED NOT BE ARTISTS; the participation of professional artists only serving to increase further the diversity of invention.*
> *New Epoch Art, Peter Benjamin Graham (InterACTA No 4 1990)*

4. A General Catalogue of Notation Systems

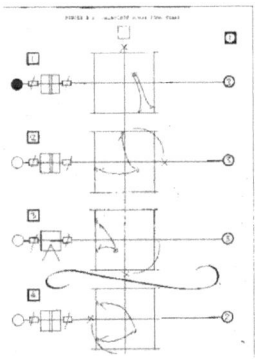

New Epoch score of Grainger Country by Peter Graham 1979

Spatial (as in, non-textual) Notation

In notation, different formats will use the same data for very different purposes. When the goal is to highlight specific relationships between elements (like distance, size, connection or differences) or stressing a point of view, nothing beats the graphical or spatial systems, a favorite of the general public for its approachable and colorful results, but also of advertisers, preachers and politicians for it allows for a great deal of manipulation.

The most common and widely used example of spatial notation is of course the map, whether physical or abstract. Thanks to the fashionable field of data visualization and the amazing tools developed in the last few years, these days we even see mixtures of both, like in this expressionist map of human poverty created with World Mapper.

Territory size shows the proportion of the world's population living in poverty in that territory.

This map is quite emphatically not the territory, but is still truthful and still a map. The natural borders are repurposed as a container for an unexpected rating value; the proportion of the world population living in poverty. Precision, though, is here sacrificed for a higher impact. If we wanted to use the data for purposes other than the denunciation of a humanitarian crisis, we would be better off with a numeric notation.

Maps are double-edged tools, for on top of manipulation, they also leave room for endless misinterpretations. In *They Rule*, a project that illuminates the invisible networks of corporate power, the human eye inevitably sees connections that don't exist. This is not the intention of the artists but, as it usually happens with maps of the underground where the layout sacrifices realism for the sake of clarity, we derive false information under the apparent but false premise of proximity.

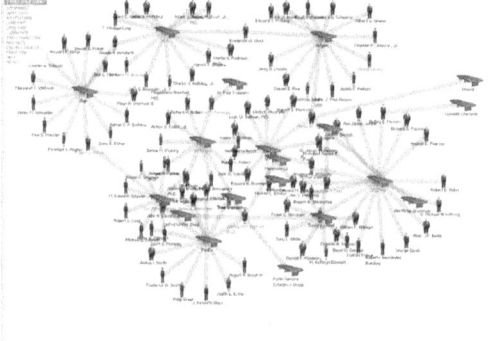

They Rule diagram of corporate relations.

Despite the high attention paid to data visualization projects nowadays, not all spatial notation serves sociocultural agendas; somewhere in between artist and spatial systems lie architectural and engineering diagrams. We see them every day, from the fire exit maps that welcome us in malls to Leonardo da Vinci's studies of the human body, though it was only after the Industrial Revolution that such kinds of notation became standarized. We will look at these forms more deeply in the Purposes for Notation chapter.

Computer Notation

A successful notation system begins with formal models of that which it wants to notate. This is an intellectual exercise we've been performing from punching cards to HTML5, with varying levels of abstraction and it is the task that Vladimir Stepanov put himself to when trying to register the movements of the Imperial ballerinas with absolute precision. It is hard not to wonder what such a visionary would have done with a laptop on hand but it might not be far away from the dancing robot that awaits the reader a few chapters away.

In certain ways, most code is not so different from formal scientific notation, though the binary number system uses powers of two instead of powers of 10, and the computer doesn't understand what it interprets. Some people are capable of writing straight into computer code without running it, the way Beethoven wrote music without hearing it but the opposite will not occur. An image file might as well be the notation of the image it generates but, while only a machine can render it visible to us, the machine itself remains blind to what is in it. That is, until the Singularity.

It is constructive to remember that computers don't read between the lines but they do fill in the blanks. A machine is literal, not metaphorical, and is always going to interpret the code exactly the way it was written, whether it serves our purpose or not. There are specific semantic interpretations of what certain things mean, and there may be indeterminism as a hidden part.

This interesting problem (and its consequences) are illustrated in a subtle difference between the almost-identical visual programming languages *Pure Data* and *Max/MSP*[1].

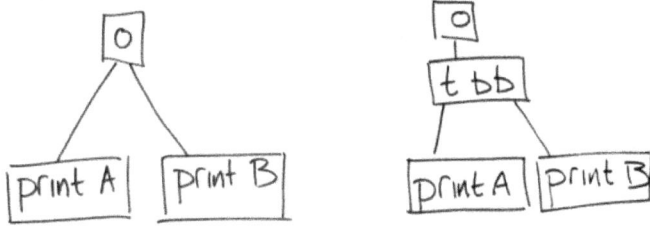

Two simple Pure Data or Max patches. The left example has indeterminacy as a Pure Data patch, the standard solution is shown on the right with a t b b ("trigger bang bang") object.

A very simple patch is created with a single bang that is connected to two print objects labelled A and B. This is a definite computer program and will be run by the computer without any further intervention by a person to implement the finer details. In Pure Data, two outcomes are possible. They are:

```
A: bang
B: bang
```

and

```
B: bang
A: bang
```

In the technical explanation of the semantics of *Pure Data* patches, it is stated that the choice that is made between these two options is purely nondeterministic, there is no decision. In the current implementation, there is a specific determination; the connection that was created first is used first. But this is not part of the program specification and later implementations might change this. This is an interesting way for the system to fill in the blanks and can be misused by deleting and then recreating connections to make them newer and thus used later. As indicated above, the trigger object can be used to determine which event should happen in what order.

In *Max/MSP*, the filling in of the blanks is more literal. The blank space and the position of objects are semantically significant. The object to the right is fed data first. So in that system, the result will always be:

```
B: bang
A: bang
```

Stay put: the trickiness of computer notation will be described in more detail further within these pages.

---

1. See the discussion:
   http://en.wikipedia.org/wiki/Visual_programming_language

PURPOSES FOR NOTATION

But suicides have a special language.
Like carpenters they want to know which tools.
They never ask why build...
Ann Sexton

After looking at some basic terminology and clarifying some rules, forms and phenomena of notation systems, we finally get to the point where we can discuss "why build." Or, in other words, for what human enterprises is notation useful and interesting? This we have discovered so far: the purposes can be numerous.

To Understand

In essence all forms of notation transport data from one medium to another; and at the core of every transition there is the mind being both actor and audience. For that reason, our first example of notation has an audience of one, with the purpose of creating a personal overview through ordering, clarifying and reflecting on a complex idea, notion or topic: the infamous *note to self*.
We are all familiar enough with this concept, and it is fair to say it is not learned but intuitive: the universal instinct to write down a list of representative values and look at it, in search for something that we haven't seen yet. Since the primary purpose is not to communicate an idea to a larger group but to create a broadened understanding for one's own self, we can get away with freestyle, as long as we can read it later. Interestingly enough, our freestyle has a penchant for lists and diagrams.
When the process extends beyond one's own eyebrows to involve other people, the notation must be legible. Used effectively, doodles can work as well as very detailed maps, if they are sufficient in the context to organise the group and coordinate their activities. A group of various specialists needing to be coordinated will have few pieces of terminology in common, so some structures that can be individually annotated for each specialist need to be found.
A storyboard contains instructions for moving camera and objects to coherently help a film team establish what is going to happen, and what they need to do. This notation system aims at giving (technical) instructions as well as an overview. The various specialists will however use the same system in various ways: while the camera crew will use it to group shots by angles to minimise camera changes, the costume team

Thoughts on Notation

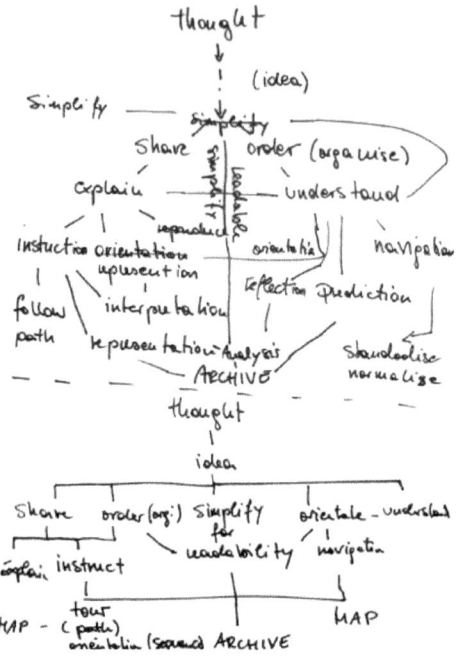

One of the stages of this chapter being developed.

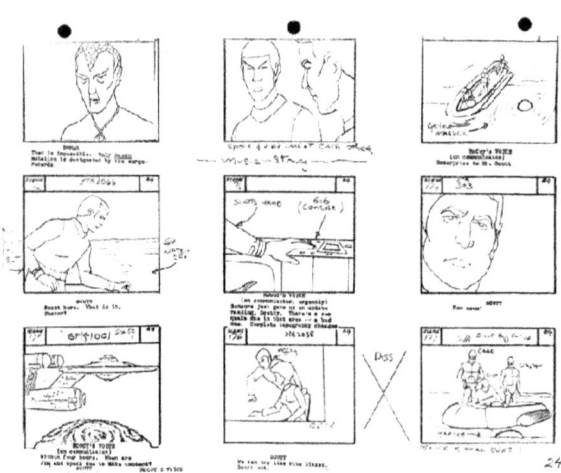

A sample storyboard with recognisable characters.

5. Purposes for Notation

will use it to check that all pieces are ready to go and will coordinate with continuity to ensure that the right stains are in the right places.

To Navigate

Often data becomes so complex that we need a process of compression to get an overview of the whole system. The most literal notation systems are probably maps.
Taking the whole world and reducing it to a globe to be held in one's hands, or projecting it flat to be kept in a book, spread on a table, or hung on a wall allows us to identify the relationships between the different elements that configure our planet. It is valuable in a way could not be gathered through lists of meters, kilometres and other terrestrial conventions of land.

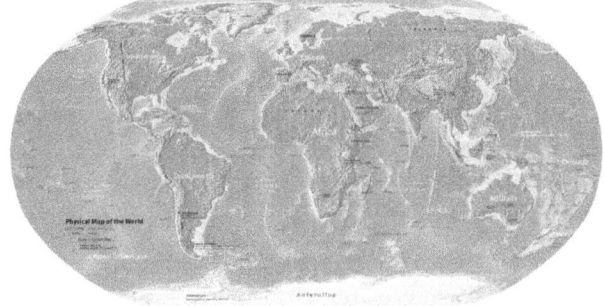

A relatively classical two dimensional representation of the planet and its physical features.

In order to make one's way through a territory, a mud map scratched in the dirt showing the trails and trees as navigation may suffice. We have a way with maps; even confronted with a path to climb a rock wall with the safety bolts indicated, or the position of waypoints in an orienteering race, maps are universally understood or at least easily learned. Let's not forget, the use of maps is learnt and their standard elements are soaked in cultural and political context, such as which way is "up," or what region is at the center.
More conveniently, maps also allow for multiple layers of data to overlay and juxtapose in engaging ways without redundancy, as in collecting traffic networks, noise levels and rubbish collecting patterns in the same city, or studying and monitoring human movement in public spaces such as malls or airports. The more complex the ideas, actions or processes are, the stronger the need for notation (and/or the higher the level of abstraction). Sometimes the creation of a certain mapping system requires a lot of effort to develop an idea that looks simple in

retrospect. Consider the multitude of globe projections onto two dimensional maps that have been created for a multitude of purposes. The precise distortion of the Mercator projection allows angles to be read from the map and used immediately for navigation. However a different type of map is needed to compare surface areas across a map's surface. Anyone interested in this matter can dive into the extraordinary *How to Lie with Maps*, by Mark Monmonier. We'll call it dragons for the sake of this volume.

When the lands of unmanageable proportion are symbolic values, we tend toward the kind of compression that characterizes scientific notation systems. Much of science consists in digging and exploiting patterns. For augmenting precision in evaluation, a very large amount of data must be collected, requiring a high level of compression. For instance, Euler's Second Law of motion states that "the rate of change of angular momentum L is equal to the sum of the external moments M" but, for calculating purposes, it is better used through this formula:

$$\mathbf{M} = \frac{d\mathbf{L}}{dt}$$

Universality facilitates the cross-pollination of scientific ideas: as long as we can show that the axioms are true and stay within the range of applicability (physics, economics, electrical circuits), we can use a formula for many other purposes without even having to understand what's in it. The process of abstraction from specific problems to a notation allows us to apply abstract and general results and techniques that have been proven to be true without having to be proven in each specific field individually. We can use the same techniques to solve this differential equation whether it be describing momentum, population growth or the amplitude of an oscillating circuit.

For calculations, one often uses so-called Scientific Notation which is based on powers of the base number 10 (as opposite to the binary system, which is based on the powers of 2 and only uses the numbers 0 and 1) and researchers use it to navigate through very large (or very small) numbers. Instead or writing 1,230,000,000 and 0.00000000123 we write 1.23e9 and 1.23e-9 and have a more concise and easily comprehensible way to talk about these values.

More importantly, notations need to convert concepts with reluctant contours and unstable shadows into managable units, what Leibniz liked to call "ideal entities," and then proceed to pin them down. The examples range from Stephen Wolfram's notation for two state cellular automata to Georg Cantor's transfinite numbers, of which ω (omega) is the lowest and (equivalently) $\aleph_0$ (Aleph-null) the first with a series of Alephs above that. In both cases, symbolic values are used as a variable

5. Purposes for Notation

to find out more about what it is when it is too messy, too big or too distant for us to see, and are subject to calculations and logical processes that reveal the edges of those dark spots. Indeed, there is still a lack of clarity about something called the Continuum Hypothesis exploring the way that infinities interrelate, a dark spot that may be more delineable in the future.

To Share and Archive

Any kind of archiving project offers a very specific kind of problem: preserving information in a way that could be meaningful for future generations – those unknown entities with crazy devices and impossible slang. For a culture fond of tradition, there is a lot to remember: processes, ideas, concepts, designs. While the mechanics of archiving material should be simple enough - reduce the work to its atomic indivisible parts without renouncing any of its content - institutions are plagued with questions of authenticity, readability and universality. Mainly: How much can you reduce a work before turning it into another work? What quotation system will remain stable enough so that we can interpret it in the years ahead? How do we ensure that the code and tools for interpretion will remain in our culture?

This has become a significant problem in the realm of electronic art over the past few decades as devices become obsolete or corrode, replacement parts become unavailable and data formats unreadable. Scientific and everyday data is not immune. The data captured on the first Viking missions to Mars in the 1970s is largely lost to unstoppable bit rot[1], piles of self-burnt CDs and DVDs are succumbing to ultraviolet radiation as we speak.

Whether or not a form of notation lends itself to archiving depends on a large variety of factors, often dependent upon the length of time that one would like to think of as being culturally relevant to keep the information. Notations can easily become as complex as the thing they are trying to simplify.

Gerhard Dirmoser maps collections by using diagrammatic representations of exhibitions. The diagram above shows material from an exhibition at the Nordico[2] in Linz which exhibits 600 pieces that have personal stories attached to them. He reduces it to a diagram, abstracting the structures in the show by using verbs that appear in the texts of the personal stories and created co-relation between them in 4 sections; collecting, exhibiting, remembering and (story) telling. He also integrates a timeline around the periphery of the diagram. This combination of several diagrammatic techniques to give a meaningful

Gerhard Dirmoser's "Erzähl uns Linz" diagram.

whole is one of his characteristics.

To Engineer

When designing a device to be built, the engineer or designer aims to include enough information to allow the device to be built exactly as it has been planned and analysed. A high level of detail is required in order to let the engineer know that the calculations relating to strength, movements, voltage, etcetera will hold. Engineering notation also uses aggregation, inheritance and functional hierarchies in order to most carefully and clearly communicate the design. Such precision in design often calls for a mixture of spatial and scientific systems at a number of levels of detail. Electrical circuit boards, for instance, are interesting kind of maps where every element describes its role in a symbolic but also explicitly physical fashion. Similarly, some computer software such as *Pure Data* use notation that both describes and generates the output; here the map and the territory are in some way interchangeable.

An engineer will use a variety of notations to describe the object being planned and built. Two-dimensional projections of the thing being built are common. These will correspond to some agreed-upon standards, whether they use the notation of technical drawing for steel parts, or the standards for multiple cross sections in boatbuilding. Mathematical notation will be used to take the dimensions of the object and calculate important properties such as the righting moment, strength of beams, the damping effects of an inductor. Every system will be chosen so as to have a sufficient level of detail for all concerned.

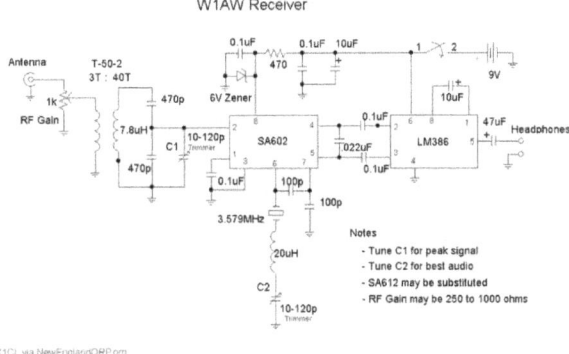

A schematic diagram of a radio receiver.

Paradoxically, engineers and inventors also archive their ideas to protect them from being used or copied, describing a process, product or design so it may not be exploited without permission in the future. Patents, for instance, are intended to describe an innovation so as to allow people to use it, but always licensing it from the patent owner, whilst exposing the details of functionality for educational purposes. Because of its economical (or simply antisocial) ambition, the language is often as imprecise as the law allows for, trying to embrace as many uses or variations of a given process or structure as there could be, such as Apple Corporation's infamous rounded corners.

To Economise

A common motivation that appeals to all disciplines is efficiency in time and space. It this case, compression is not only the process but also the goal, whether to archive material in the smallest possible space, or to

Thoughts on Notation

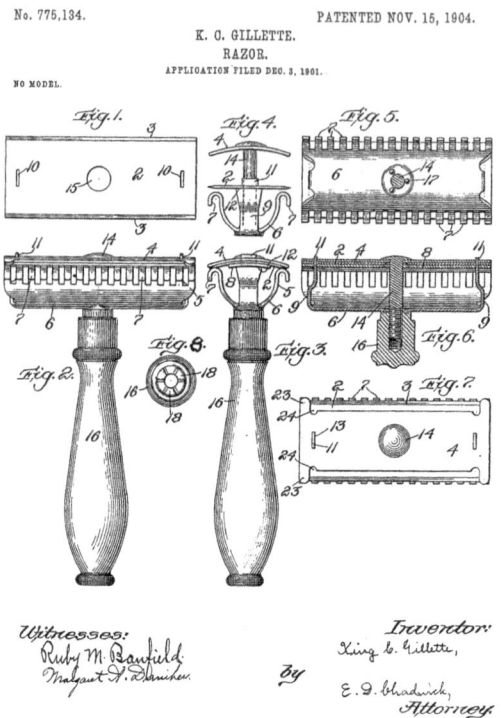

Gillette's patent drawing of the Razor, 1904

transmit or record it in the smallest amount of time. Tachygraphy naturally comes to mind, a symbolic writing method used by notators along the centuries in a variety of machines. The history of algebraic notation – from the first *rhetorical* face where all calculations were described verbally, to the last *symbolic* one where every element is a symbolic replacement of the rhetoric premises – could potentially be studied as a process of language reduction, where the system of notation itself has been boiled down to its most concentrated form, always without losing any of its information.

This is also the challenge we witness while reading the algebraic-like proposals of Cartesian logics, or in Ludwig Wittgenstein's *Tractatus Logico-Philosophicus*, whose original name was *Der Satz* (commonly translated as proposition, sentence, phrase or set, but also *leap*).

In computational theory, the business of stuffing as much data in the smallest amount of time/space can be discussed as Kolmogorov

5. Purposes for Notation

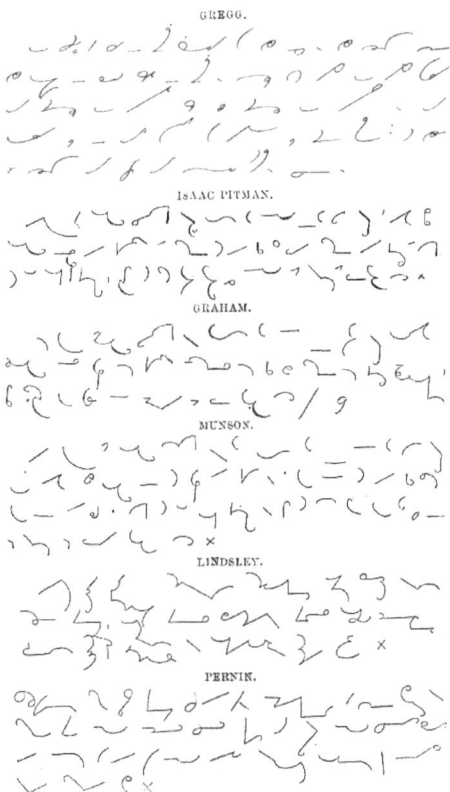

Eclectic shorthands: The Lord's Prayer in Gregg and a variety of 19th-century shorthand systems

complexity, a measure of the computational resources that are needed to specify the original object, not as a thing, but as the way, the recipe, to build or make that thing. In any case, readability is reduced not transformed; the notation requires to be transformed back into its original system state by the reader through reading and some form of implementation. In many such systems, the context of the notation is very rich, enabling a small movement or subtle difference in sign to transport a very significant difference in meaning. Shorthand writing is a complex and highly differentiated collection of systems to perform this compact notation of spoken to written text. While many standards have existed, many groups and even individuals develop their own versions so as to most economically store their specific types of text.

Thoughts on Notation

"Reality Shift" in use in Maubeuge, France.

To Analyse

The reduction of a complex system to a notated, abstracted one, allows a more direct analysis, ignoring details that are not appropriate or relevant for the analysis being undertaken. We take the interactive maze *Reality Shift* from Time's Up as an illustrating example.

The desire was to have a grid of vertical cylinders into which a person could step, rotate, and then step out of in another direction. The possibilities to step in to and out of the cylinders, combined with the way that the cylinders move, should be constructed in a way that led to a labyrinth to be explored. A grid of 16 cylinders arranged in four rows of four was decided upon. For mechanical simplicity, groups of four cylinders were chosen as the connected units.

In order to analyse the options of the system, a diagram that displays the ways in which 16 cylinders that rotate around their own axis in groups of four was used. These diagrams ignore the material and mechanics of the labyrinth, weight, friction and dimensions. The diagrams below show how the cylinders work with the possible motions through the cylinders in various positions being shown in red (light grey), the rotations in blue (dark grey). Such a notation becomes a necessity when starting to think about more than four cylinders working at a time.

5. Purposes for Notation

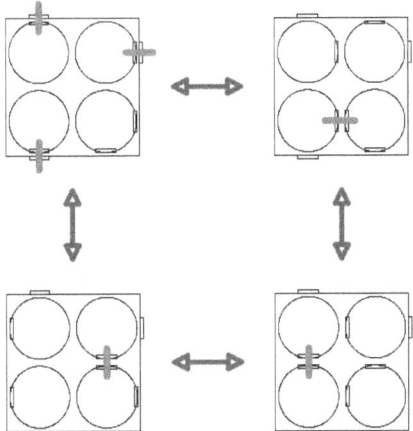

Motions and arrangements in a 2x2 block of rotating cylinders.

Several decisions led to this particular collection of cylinder arrangements. Users should only be able to leave and enter each block in a given "initial" state, so that when the block was exited, it was ready for a person to enter it again. With the rectilinear arrangement of the cylinders, it was chosen that people would only move in the four directions, and that the rotations would have four places to allow movement, each separated by 90 degrees of rotation. Safety was a concern; if the doors moved in contrary directions to one another, this would create a chopping action when the doors closed. Thus adjacent cylinders move in clockwise-anticlockwise direction pairs so as to remove this danger. This reinforced the need for a rectilinear arrangement on a square grid as opposed to a triangular or other arrangement. The analysis ensures that it is possible to move through the block between each of the entry-exit doors. It was found that one cylinder having two open sections (lower right in the diagram) was needed in order to make this possible in a nontrivial fashion.

The second diagram shows the paths it is possible to take in order to navigate through all 16 cylinders arranged in a grid. The complete labyrinth is drawn in its initial state.

This notation had the purpose to predict and communicate movement sequences for an installation piece. While the paths through are simple when seen independently of the movements, the amount of rotary motion needed to get from one cylinder to the next led to directional confusion and a satisfactory labyrinth experience.

Thoughts on Notation

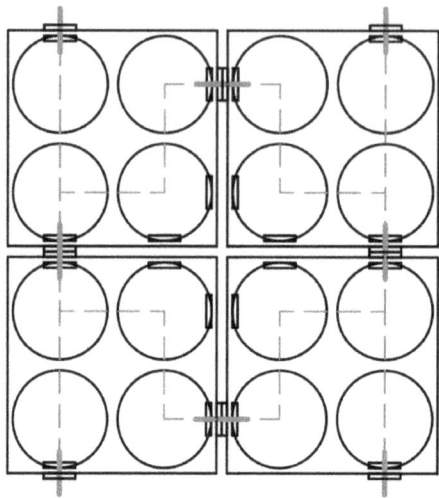

Possible paths through the labyrinth "Reality Shift."

To Interpret

An interesting example of interpretation can be seen in the practice of rebuilding or re-implementing old electronic art pieces, especially in various code forms. The process, to take a concrete hypothetical example, involves taking a carefully engineered piece of video hardware and analysing the process, developing an abstracted notation of the important properties and processes of the original electronic piece and working out what is and what is not important about it; hand soldered and wirewrapped circuitry, for instance, is unimportant, the treatment of scanlines vital. Then the abstracted version of the piece, notated in whichever form seems most appropriate, is used to implement the piece once again in a chosen programming environment.

The new piece is in some sense a copy of the original, yet it is very distinct, being built on a very different substrate. One interpretation is that the code is an abstraction of the electronics, one turtle standing upon another, a different point of view has the two turtles standing next to one another, both being a level of detail upon which the same turtle, the actual piece of art itself, can stand.

The purpose of the notation is to derive the core functionality and

aesthetics of the original piece in order to allow a new interpretation. A similar process happens when musicians decide to interpret one another's work. They decide what is important, whether it is a melody or other "hook" line, the rhythm, the chord progression or the text. Devo's interpretation of the Rolling Stones "Satisfaction" took very little of the original to produce a vitally new interpretation; other interpretations, for instance by "tribute bands," are closer to the original to the point of near interchangeability. A similar process takes place when music is arranged for different instrumentation and the sustained notes of a viola are left to fade or repeatedly struck on a piano.
The need to notate and obtain the core elements of a given piece in order to interpret it can be seen, on some level, to be based upon the nonexistence of another form of notation from which the original piece was created. In general, notation for interpretation serves the main purpose of preparing a communicating of a set of rules, commands, steps, etc. with the core intention of production rather than reproduction.

To Disguise

Both the most photogenic and elusive use of notation, this is the art of obscuring or concealing data in order to transmit it without revealing its contents or simply, without being seen. Many today, from international men of mystery to libertarian cryptopartiers, use encryption to protect their transmissions from eavesdroppers, or steganography to bury messages in inconspicuous carriers and create necessary paths of private communication in our hypersurveilled society.
Cryptography's most notorious icon in the western world, the Enigma cipher machine, was designed to perform one alphabetic substitution cipher after another, making it nigh upon impossible for the enemy to decrypt the message, or so time-consuming that even the correct resolution of the message would be useless. In the original model, letters are scrambled by a set of consecutive rotatable wheels that change position with each encoded letter.
Not so different from the Enigma, Tor (the onion router) allows for anonymous browsing and package exchange between people. In this case what is concealed is not the message but the sender, creating a maze of ever rotating IPs that make it difficult for organisms like the RIAA or fascist governments to know for sure who is doing what and where.
The rules of this system are obvious: both receiver and producer of the notation must share the key to the code, otherwise the material will be lost like tears in the rain. About the complexity of the key, it depends

Thoughts on Notation

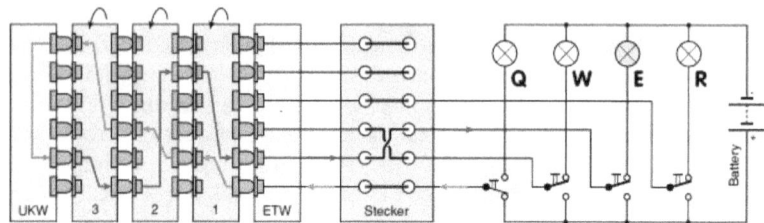
Simplified circuit diagram of a 3-wheel Service Enigma

mostly on the danger itself. How smart or well-equipped is the enemy? How much do we care? The most secure method, a one-time pad, cannot be reused (as its name suggests) and is therefore complex to transport. A simple method might be easily transported, but is also easily broken. It is all about choosing a suitable level of notation, to select the appropriate tool.

To Notate

We come to the end of our necessarily finite list of possible purposes for notation. In the next few chapters we will look at some of the properties of notation, about the levels of abstraction, readability and interpretability. Armed with the places notation can be used and the forms it can take, let us venture into some ideas about the very structure of notation.

1. The Long Now Foundation investigates many of the responses to this problem, dealing with questions of information deterioration and semantics that reach across cultural traditions. See http://longnow.org/
2. Website: http://www.nordico.at/

THE AGENCY OF THE MAP

All notation partakes of one of two formats: the map or the tour. In a classic article about how residents of New York City describe their flats, Linde and Labov (1975) discovered that all the descriptions fell into only two types, The first type is some variation of the following: "The bedroom is next to the kitchen"; the second type sounds like this: "You turn right and come into the living room." These are labelled, respectively, the "map" and the "tour." In this particular study, only three per cent of the people interviewed chose to describe their flats using the "map" style. All the rest chose the "tour" style.

These two types of descriptions, the map and tour, illustrate a longstanding and critical difference in how people understand their environment: seeing vs. going, presenting a tableau vs. organising someone's movements. The tour is a more aggressive dialogue between person and object. It limits choices and insists on keeping to a specific path. It makes sense that it would dominate people's descriptions of their flats. They want us to see their homes as a specific series of impressions in a particular sequence. The tour includes effects ("you will see . . ."), limits ("there is a wall"), possibilities ("there is a door"), and directives ("look to your left"). The tour produces a representation of the flat in our minds as the resident wants us to experience it. It brings the flat into social existence. This is the tour's agency.

The map form of the description affords more choice. It is heavy with positional pointers: "this is next to that," or "this is before that," but is lacking in action or performance. The resident is saying to the guest, "Here is the floor plan. You may move through it anyway you wish." The resident interacts with the map as she presents the tour. From it, she selects a path and narrates its landmarks. These landmarks and all possible paths are potential in the map. This is the map's agency. As notational practices, then, both maps and tours are dialogues about a performance, but with different ways of directing, modifying or augmenting an experience.

Agency is a human quality. It refers to any action intentionally performed by someone and understood by others. Notations cannot generate their own agency because they cannot have intentions. They are not conscious. However, anthropologists have shown that objects do contain implicit messages that are put there by people, and that can direct, modify or augment the actions of others. Agency in notation inhabits a world of ambiguity and indeterminacy, frustrating our efforts to grasp it as if it were concrete and fixed. Like the particle and the wave in quantum physics, the notation and its agency coexist in the same moment but are apprehended separately. When we observe the notation, its agency disappears and when we observe the agency the notation disappears.

Knitting Notations

We experience notations as representations of different kinds of performances. These focus on the important places or moments in a event and leave out the unimportant ones. Many different kinds of time-based experiences can be described in maps and tours. Take, for example, the notations for knitting a garment. Cleaned, separated and spun into yarn, wool is knitted into garments by various techniques. The experience of knitting a garment unfolds in time and space. One creates the space as one knits one stitch at a time, until the garment is complete. Knitting a single sock takes about 20 hours and involves making 13,000 individual stitches. Knitting a man's jumper takes over 200 hours and involves making 132,000 stitches. In both cases, one starts out on the journey with a single stitch. The stitch pattern changes from time to time, as almost all garments require shaping. Holes for arms may require dividing the work. Heels need special techniques to create the 'turn'. The journey ends by stitching the various pieces together, or closing up the tube.

This is a representation of the stitch pattern for a sleeveless vest, designed by the British fabric artist Kim Hargreaves, as one would find it in contemporary charted European and American instructions for a patterned garment. This is a map constructed on a grid where each box represents one stitch. The vest builds using only two stitches, a knit stitch that results in a loop where the yarn pushes forward and indicated by a empty grid square, and a purl stitch where the yarn pulls backward and represented by a square with a dot in it. These symbols vary in different European languages but the stitches themselves are ancient and universal. The alternation of these two stitches produces the brocade decoration for the vest. We can just begin to glimpse the brocade in the overall pattern of dots. The notation begins in the lower right corner and moves row by row, "as an ox plows a field," to the top left. This particular map superimposes the boundaries for seven different sizes. There is also a gap between the bottom edge pattern and the chest pattern in which one knits row after row until a specific length is completed.

One could fashion a garment using only this map. Doing so affords the knitter many more choices of how to accomplish the pattern. However, generally European and American knitting instructions also include a

6. The Agency of the Map

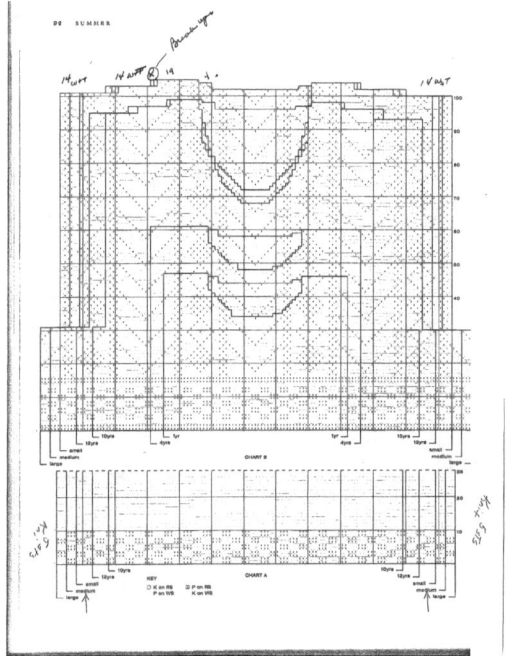

Knit pattern for a vest in modern Anglo-Saxon style.

tour of the territory of the garment that uses only words to describe the space. Such notation, like all tours, uses code and arranges its elements in classes, objects and properties.

Like all tours it removes options from the knitter. It chooses between top down and bottom up. It assumes that the front and back will be knitted separately and sewn together when completed. Knitters could knit both pieces together as a wide, round tube until the armholes. It invokes knowledge of landmarks that are specific to the territory of vests, jumpers and cardigans, such as side vents, armholes, right sides and wrong sides (WS), garter stitch and straight stitch (st st). Finally, it connects to the map with its references to Chart A and Chart B. The tour of the vest is a document of the designer's knitting practices. Most craft knitters will follow her tour to the letter. Fabric artists and experienced crafters will use the tour as an introduction to the territory of the garment, study the map, and then adjust the tour to their own practices.

Notation can be localized. The preceding pattern reflects European

Thoughts on Notation

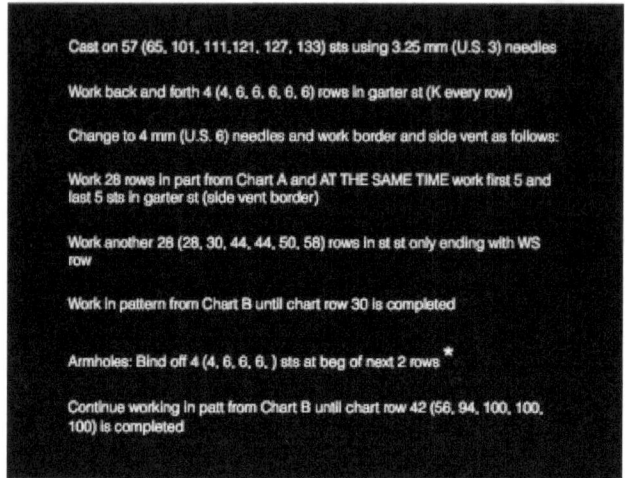

The tour notation for knitting the back of the vest, translating the map above to a list of instructions.

and American conventions. In Japanese designs, we find the map and the tour combined. In the example shown below, a western fabric artist added the annotations in English to help non-Japanese readers interpret the patterns. The map of the garment begins in the same place, the lower right. Instead of a grid, we see the external and internal boundaries of the territory only. The figure on the left is the back of the vest, while the one on the right is front. The knitter knows that both halves of the back or front are knitted together. One then sews the front and back together. The lines in the lower half of the vest indicate where the stitch pattern changes: x number of stitches for y number of rows repeated z number of times. A character indicates the particular kind of stitch. The characters in the band at the bottom of the vest translate as "1x1 ribbing." The numbers separated by hyphens indicate changes in the number of stitches per row when shaping the arm holes and neck. Binding off a stitch reduces the number of stitches in a row. So, for example 2-2-2 means "every two rows, bind off two stitches at the arm hole edge and do this twice." Then the next instruction is 2-1-5, or "every two rows, bind off one stitch and do this five times." This continues until the knitter reaches the top of the armhole.

The chart patterns of the vest are rendered as a formula rather than boxes on a grid. The amount of information available in the representation of the vest is dramatically reduced and more knowledge of getting around is shifted to the knitter. For example, the knitter

6. The Agency of the Map

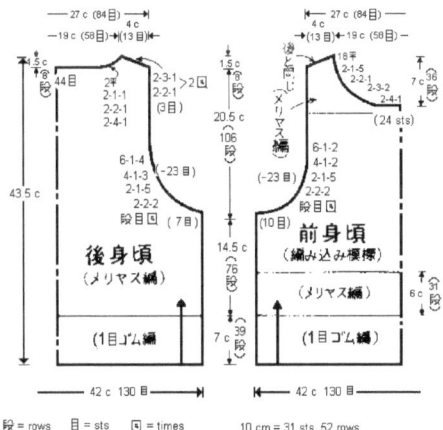

Japanese knitting notation with western annotations.

"knows" that 1x1 ribbing is always knitted with needles two sizes smaller than the rest of the garment. The knitter "understands" how increases and decreases in stitch counts affect the overall shape of the vest. This notation is far more map-like and requires more background knowledge and experience to orient oneself and reach one's goal. This is not necessarily more liberating than the notation for the vest. Decoding of the path through particularly complex patterns, like the vest, would confound all but the most experienced knitter aware of the intricacies of Japanese knitting notation.

The Agency of Notation Systems

Maps, tours, and patterns are not unique, singular objects. Instead, each must be seen as a class comprised of sets of places, paths, or stitches. Therein lies a further complication to understanding their agency: when we focus on notation as class, specific political, competitive and conflictive meaning immediately arise. These meanings are intentional, yet tacit. The author produces the notation to influence the performance of subsequent actors. Deleuze and Guattari (1987) first brought attention to this quality of sets in the discussion of *assemblage*, one of their abstract machines through which large numbers of people act out practices that produce similar results or artifacts. An assemblage is specifically a desiring machine. That is, people use it to gratify their separate desires that nevertheless produce similar outcomes. All machines portray knowledge as occupying two different states simultaneously as a whole and as the parts that comprise the whole. Analogously, we understand bodies as wholes, or as parts. When understood as wholes, the body occupies one kind of space and time. When understood as parts, the body occupies a different kind of space and time. The whole is animate. It moves, and in the process of doing so occupies or constitutes space. The parts are inanimate. The threshold that permits the parts to function as a body is their cooperation. More importantly, the specific way the parts work together to be or act in the world distinguishes one body from another. With notation, the whole is a functioning system that produces space, and often time as well, while the parts are the symbolic objects and their properties. It is the coherence of these objects with each other, their "cooperation," that permits the notation as a whole to function. Since that notation is the fulfillment of the desire of the actor to realize the performance of the author, notation is a desiring machine.

The author and actor are not on equal footing here. The politics of the notational assemblage tilt decidedly in favor of the author. Maps and tours can illustrate this. In the tour format, the author specifies each turn and the distance between turns. The actor has little choice but to follow. The author remains in control throughout. The map permits the actor more latitude in choosing a path to the goal. The author of the map relinquishes control over parts of the process.

There are several ways that authors exert control through the choice of specific notational symbols. Every symbol has a history. It may have been produced idiosyncratically and attributed to a specific author. It may have been transferred from a different notational system. It may result from a misappropriation or misinterpretation of an existing symbol. Symbols may be associated with a specific body of work that occurred in a notorious performance, forever connecting those symbols to that event. Deleuze and Guattari find the ad hoc nature of the parts of the assemblage fascinating. These multiple origins result in no one symbol dominating the set. In fact, the relative equanimity among the symbols permits the author greater flexibility in rendering the work. This equanimity is only relative, however. Some symbols are simply constructed and refer to common, often repeated actions. Others are more complexly constructed that others, requiring greater interpretation by actors, diminishing the control of the author.

The collection of symbols is also a captured flow of elements whose origins and intended trajectories may be quite different from each other. Yet, these trajectories exist and co-exist with the ad hoc collection that constitutes the notational system. This capture and redirection of elements to the author's purposes is both a creative and

6. The Agency of the Map

destructive act. It is creative because it brings about the birth of a notation that more precisely describes the indescribable. It is a destructive act because it wrenches elements from the existing context, generating new connotations for them, and thereby rendering them more ambiguous and diffuse than they were originally. To know the history of these symbols is to know, or to have personally experienced, the history of the authors. To not know the history is to perform the work blind to the historical resonances of its creation, and therefore, to perform only a portion of the work.

Creative work is embedded in sentimental communities. These are networks of authors, actors, and audiences who share a similar commitment to sensory and aesthetic preferences in the choice of materials, techniques, creative practices, performance venues, tonalities, messages, and originality. Sentimental communities develop according to a specific historical arc. They arise out of the cooperation of an initial set of authors. They grow and mature by the addition of actors and audiences who invest in maintaining the original preference set, especially in competition with other sentimental communities. They decline and disappear as the commitments of newer generations of actors and audiences find their voice in other communities. Transformational movements outside themselves, like romanticism or modernism, sometimes shape these sentimental communities.

The agency of the notational systems engenders debate between authors, actors, and audience within the community, driving development of newer forms. These systems police the boundary between one sentimental community and another, especially when both communities are employing similar media or competing for the patronage of similar audience. The systems also lend coherence to the community. Entry into the community begins with learning the notational system, after mastering some basic techniques, and replicating 'classic' works using the system. One signals rejection of the community by establishing a different notational system. Transforming the community is accomplished as much through the reorganization, clarification and elaboration of the notations as it is by creating seminal performances.

The agency of notational systems revolves around implicit messages left upon them by authors to influence the performances of actors. People employ notational systems as desiring machines to realize imitative and novel versions of creative work. With the addition of an audience, the notational system brings the sentimental community into existence.

Thoughts on Notation

TURTLES ALL THE WAY DOWN

"We don't live on a ball revolving around the Sun," she said, "we live on a crust of earth on the back of a giant turtle."
Wishing to humor the woman Russell asked, "And what does this turtle stand on?"
"On the back of a second, still larger turtle," was her confident answer.
"But what holds up the second turtle?" he persisted, now in a slightly exasperated tone.
"It's no use, young man," the old woman replied, "it's turtles all the way down."
Stephen Hawking, A Brief History of Time.

In the Foreword we mentioned the "bottomless stack of turtles" effect[1]. Levels of increasing abstraction, notational accuracy, arrayed one on top of another. Yet not all these levels of focus are equally useful for the expression, discussion, or transmission of a particular piece of work to a specific audience. Some levels of abstraction are insufficiently detailed, consisting more of an evocative "description" than a functional notation. Other levels may be so needlessly detailed that they no longer allow a human reader to understand and meaningfully interpret a work. Yet those layers may be much more appropriate for machine readers (computers), which can interpret much greater amounts of input, faster, and with more accuracy. This of course depends upon the format of the notation: not all deep levels of description are necessarily formal and are thus possibly not readable by a computer. Finally the turtle-descent begins to beg the question: at which layer of detail does a notation becomes the work itself? Put philosophically: when, especially in consideration of interactive and digital content, does the map become equal to the territory?[2] Or at least structurally indistinguishable from it? And which level is most useful in any given context for getting something done? For every domain – indeed for each work – this question may be answered differently.

We consider the extremes of detail-level as Dragons, notation levels too abstract or too specific to be useful as communication of the desired expression or information. Of particular fire-breathing danger is natural language as a representational system: insidiously slippery, adaptable to all levels of detail, shaping reality and its relationships, yet demanding creative and imaginative effort to interpret. A more paranoid approach might spot the possibilities of Goedelian inconsistency in any system capable of notating arithmetic. But in between the dragons of too little and too much is a rich landscape of space and time based notational

Thoughts on Notation

systems to explore. Not too hard, not too soft, it's just right.

Different types of notation systems will be most appropriate and most useful to different groups of readers. At the most simplistic level, a division between human beings (with our limitations of perceptual speed and accuracy) and machines (with their limited powers of inference, adaptation, or change) becomes relevant. Within the human group there are many useful distinctions such as age, training, role (such as creator, interpreter, or consumer) and cultural tradition. Within the machine readers of notation, one might need to consider practical details such as operating system, installed software, system architecture and performance. At the interface between machines and humans there is an entire specialized category of notation systems - computer programming languages - varying depending on factors such as purpose, relative readability to one side or the other (aka high or low level languages), information philosophy and aesthetics.

Especially informationally dense time-based media benefit from using different notation systems at particular timescales. A song might be depicted at the highest level by broad lines, arcs, and markings equating to the emotional and dramatic shape of its sections, on the level of seconds by a chord chart, at a second-by-second level by a musical score detailing every (or at least almost every) note, and at an even finer granularity (fractions of milliseconds) by a continuous line expressing the waveform that is created by a performance of the music, a line precise enough to reproduce the sounds themselves, with computer software and hardware.

Sameness

At some level we feel that there is a certain level of *structural isomorphism* ("iso" meaning same, "morphism" meaning shape) and below this level there are further degrees of refinement that do not get closer to the original, only examine it in further detail. In software we see this quite explicitly with the level of source code for a given program being structurally isomorphic to the program being run. Deeper below we get the compiled binary, the microcode in the CPU and deeper into electronics - this gives us more detail, but does not define the program more explicitly (unless we are interested in the effects of cosmic radiation induced errors in the CPU as they bubble up and cause errors in computer results, which can be of interest to certain areas of research and development). Above this level the notation leaves aspects open that are defined more closely as we move down the turtles.

It is also worth noting that there are certain types of description that are equivalent. As we will see below, we can regard a suitably dense series of values and the mathematical equation of the curve passing through them is equivalent, as we can pass from the values to the equation by interpolation or curve fitting and back by calculating values explicitly. As these levels of description are equivalent, we can talk about equivalent turtles and raise the question of translation.

It may well be that the idea of translating across only makes sense below this level of structural isomorphism, but the answer remains open. Below that level there are definite ideas of being the same. However, once again looking ahead to the example of a robot choreography below, a sequence of key frames can be represented as numbers indicating the position of the various parts of the robot, 3D models of the robot, numbers indicating the value of the various robot actuators or detailed photographs. Then the information contained in these descriptions, these various notations, can be used to obtain the information in the others, making these descriptions equivalent in some sense.

The terms *code* and *program* continually raised problems as we conversed and discussed. At some point we believed that we had to retire the problem to the dragon department, but the following seems to be something that works. The *code*, the source code written in any computer language, can be compiled to give a working *program*. This program, when run, has certain behaviour. We regard the behaviour of the program to be the thing that we are interested in. The behaviour is the semantics of the code. The code is the notation. Two pieces of code are equivalent if they produce the same behaviour, that is, they have the same semantics. Because the code produces the program, we will talk of these as equivalent, we have introduced the term structural isomorphism to describe this.

Programs also raise other issues around uniqueness and things. The same code compiled to a program can be run simultaneously on two computers, given two things that are obviously not the same thing but are essentially the same. Two Firefox browsers on the same architecture are essentially the same. A technical way of differentiating these is to talk of instances of a program, or instantiations. This might be extended to speak of two games of chess as being instances (they are not played the same but they do start from the same state and have the same rules) or two performances of a score as being instances of that score. We raise these issues only to place a warning stick in the sand. Two performances of Chopin's *Revolutionary Étude* are instances of the same piece of music – or are they separate pieces? The human input of a performer seems to indicate that these are distinct. While this issue does not seem to be vital, there were discussions points that got carefully twisted up around these questions, so perhaps there is a dragon further down that path.

Program == Score?

Let us take this opportunity to raise another difficult question: Is the code or the patch the score? In much computer music, the composer (who may also be the performer) creates a piece of software as a patch or as code. It can be argued that this code is the score. However it is important, if not vital that the symbols in a score should have the potential to be executed by any, or at least other, software/program with any hardware, and/or any human being able to connect to the context. Chosen symbols for a score should go beyond a specific software or hardware, creating a metalanguage for interpretation. Otherwise it is not, in some sense, a score, rather it is an encoding of a specific piece and performance of music. It is a notation of it, perhaps too specific to be a score. If we take this as a given, a code or a patch is not a score any more than an efficient compression of a piece of music using advanced adaptive compression techniques is a score. Note however that a patch that implements an instrument, where the performer uses notes on paper next to the computer, is not using the patch as a score.

This also shows the importance of being aware of the point of perspective when judging the level of abstraction and precision of a notation system. Differences can exist inside and outside the notation system, but only those that are described from within (following the inner logic) exist on the inside of that specific "reality." Whatever is not part of the vocabulary of a notation system because it is not possible to produce a meaning in the system's reality has to be ignored by the judging spectator in the same way that it is ignored by the vocabulary of the system at hand.

The idea of sameness, of structural isomorphism, is somewhat difficult in the case of music, as it has to do with how we measure it. As the piece of music goes deeper in levels of description from "a piano fugue" to "the second recording of the *Goldberg Variations* by Glenn Gould" and then down to the various media with which that could be reproduced we come to ask whether there is structural isomorphism between the LP, CD and MP3 versions, or whether the version I hear on my stereo is different from that heard on yours when we play the same CD. These are difficult questions once again and we believe we hear the sound of a dragon breathing down our necks, so let's leave this particular white area on the map for later explorers to more deeply determine.

Below we will contemplate the idea of a layer of abstraction so low that a composer is able to compose a piece without hearing it ever, knowing that the instance of it when performed will match his expectations due to the cultural context and the specificity of his writing.

On a more abstract level, at a higher turtle, at the *Data Ecologies* symposium the composer and musician from the theater group *Toxic Dreams*, Michael Strohmann, posed the problem of finding ways to notate electronic music such that he could plan what he was going to do before he sat down in front of the computer. He would thus avoid the danger of slipping into the miasma, of getting lost in acoustic details and losing track of what he was initially trying to do. Finding the appropriate level of detail is an ongoing issue, especially given the capacity of a computer to allow arbitrarily deep and fine meddling with acoustic details.

Taking the example of music and scores further, we can see that the top level of description - the overall structure of a musical work - could benefit most from a "timeline" style of notation: a timescale reading (typically, at least in the west) from left to right, with height and shape of a line or form equating roughly to dramatic effect, or volume, or tension, or busy-ness. The line or shape might have textures or shapes representing the instrumentation, feeling, or density of the music in a section.

This style and granularity of notation seems most appropriate for roughly describing and analyzing a dramatic linear work such as music, theater, film, or book, though it's conceivable that as music, the timeline itself could be playable if we assume quite a lot of interpretation by the performer.

How then we might look at a similarly-scaled notation system for interaction? How do we show broad dramatic changes when a work may change over time based on user input? These problems will concern us later in the book, let's concentrate upon a non-interactive example now in order to more closely examine the ideas.

A Robot Dance Gedankenexperiment

We recently saw a robot arm performance created by Matthew Gingold, an Australian media artist, where the motions of an industrial robot arm were fluid and animistic, very much like the motions of an animated character in a cartoon. We learnt some elements about what Matthew had done and will attempt to integrate them with our other understandings of how a robot notation can work in this example looking at the various levels of description.

At the top level we have something that we might call the high level "description," often in natural language. This is perhaps not quite a notation, but we cannot see the strong line between high level description and lower level notations that might also use a lot of natural language elements.

The description might be as short as "The robots dance symmetrically and gracefully before the water cannons are turned on, whereupon they fan the water into the air." This would then be refined to more detail, for instance a small section might be "The robot's arm lowers to the left, swooping like a swallow down and parallel to the ground until it comes to an abrupt stop, pulsing slightly as though breathing." From this verbal description, that is perhaps equivalent to the written instructions in a stage play, undoubtedably a form of notation, we can begin to create something more formally written down.

We come to the mid level: "human readable" notation systems.

We imagine the various positions of the robot being like key frames in an animation, with various annotations that show the type of motion between these frames; arrows, indications of rotations, accelerations, etc. Talking with the artist, it seems that the programming occurs in a similar fashion, with a number of key frames being used as fixed positions and the robot moving in a linear fashion between them. In order to create this, an operator can position the robot manually to these key frames or the key frames can be generated in a scripting language that might also include such structures as repeating loops and offsets. In order to move from the key frames with annotations and curves to the linear programming mode, a suitable large number of key frames need to be constructed so that the series of straight lines approximate the desired curve. As an example, an industrial robot's operator has most programs around 30 lines long, Matthew's program for the dance-like performance had around 280 lines.

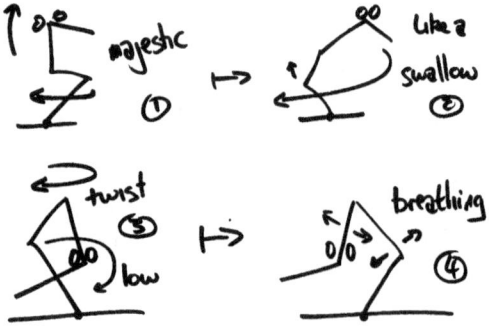

Annotated key frames of robot dance movement.

7. Turtles all the way down

$$S_1 = \begin{cases} 7 + p(t/5) \cdot 73 & t < 5 \\ 20 & 5 \leq t < 10 \\ 20 + 15 \sin\left(\frac{(t-10)}{5} \cdot 2\pi\right) & 10 \leq t < 15 \\ \vdots & \end{cases}$$

A description of movement as equations.

The problem of creating key positions is a difficult one. Industrial robots are often manipulated by a controller directly and the desired positions are created on the shop floor and stored. An animation program that simulates the motion of the robot arm allows a designer to find certain positions using the simulated robot arm. The positions can also be found by calculation or other ways.

The linear interpolation has its loops dismantled to create the lower level movement of the robot arm, with a G-code program that exactly states the types of movements that the robot arm should make. G-code is the industrial standard for Computer Numerical Control (CNC) and is used by everything from a home made 3D printer to a multiaxis redundant robot arm system for milling.

```
N1510G1X2.233Y0.641Z-0.250
N1520G1X0.561Y-2.553Z-0.250
N1530G1X-1.160Y-5.796Z-0.250
N1540G00X-1.160Y-5.796Z5.080
N1550G00X-0.558Y-5.725Z5.080
N1560G1X-0.558Y-5.725Z-0.250F150.0
N1570G1X-0.558Y-5.643Z-0.250F400.0
N1580G1X3.068Y1.209Z-0.250
N1590G1X-1.116Y1.2597-0.250
```

A sample of G-code for a simple two dimensional milling machine.

On the other hand, we could look at the movements between the key frames as a collection of parametric equations, interpolating the movement in ways that have a certain amount of smoothness using functions that the machine can implement easily. One version might use a combination of linear elements and circle segments, another might use Bezier interpolation, sine waves, or polynomials. We imagine that the motion could be created using a mathematical function that uses the parameter t corresponding to time to move along and give the resulting servo motor positions.

55

Such a piecewise function uses a collection of functions and given the appropriate tools, the mathematics involved can be analysed to enforce certain constraints on the robot servo movement. The functions can then be drawn to give a curve.

This curve shows us what movement should be created by the robot servos. One implementation of this would be to quantize the movement, to sample the mathematical functions at regular values of t and use these values to create G-code instructions. The curve would be approximately the same as the mathematical curve, with small errors due to finite exactness and round-off errors. Similarly we could take the G-code values and do some curve fitting process to find a mathematical expression that most closely approximates the series of values. One might say that the G-code and the mathematical curve are levels of details that are equivalent because we can translate from one to the other by quantisation and curve fitting - they are adjacent turtles, so to speak.

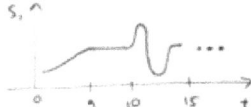

A description of movement as a curve.

As we climb down our stack of turtles, we get to what we will think of as a low level, the "machine readable code" that is perhaps too messy for humans to read on the level of complete movements of the robot.

If we imagine the control of the robot coming from a computer system, the output is some kind of data that goes to the robot control systems. A data bus is one example, sending commands to various Digital Analogue Converters (DACs) that supply values to the servo electronics, Rotary encoders (Renc) on the robot arms tell the electronics where the arms are so that the controls are accurately implemented. Feedback control systems compare the desired value and the actual value and enforce a correction to keep the system on track. If we were to have a voltage probe on the output of the DAC, we would see a curve over time that should closely approximate the curve shown above as a result of the mathematical formula notation.

At this lowest level of explanation we might find a whole spectrum of possibilities for notation utilised by engineers, mechanists and mathematicians to describe what is going on, how the instructions from the computer are translated into control values, fed to motors, the way

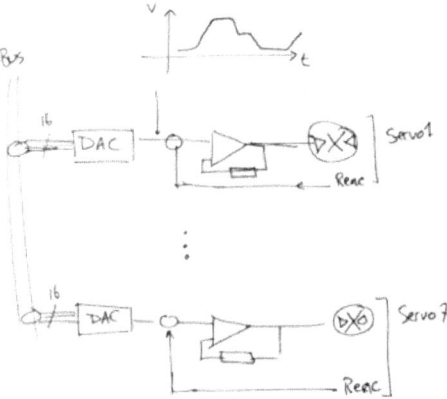

A description of movement as voltages and control electronics.

that the masses of the robot parts slow motions or enhance momentum to make certain control mechanisms impossible. The forward dynamics that tell us the motion of the robot parts in response to certain robot servo actions are a notation that summarises the mechanical device to a collection of matrices. Another mathematical model can describe the way that feedback loops lead to certain errors in the position of servos and the resulting robot arm configuration. These notations tell us about the errors and allow us to analyse the way that certain planned motions will not work the way they are planned, or that certain desired motions can be easily created using an apparently different planned motion that, with the nonlinear dynamics of the robot arm, lead us to a motion that is not as planned but perfectly as desired.

For those who want to dive deeper into the turtles, we get description for steel flexing and crystalline structure, servo motor models with magnetic effects and friction problems, sensor system noisiness and error correction, electronics design, chip and transistor design, then down further to quantum effects and the deepest layers of reality that would explode this slim volume if we were to attempt to notate them any further. There be very small dragons, but they are not ours to slay today.

---

1. http://en.wikipedia.org/wiki/Turtles_all_the_way_down
2. http://en.wikipedia.org/wiki/Map-territory_relation

Thoughts on Notation

BEETHOVEN'S DEATHBED

Picture a deaf old man, those classically piercing eyes, scribbling frantically as ideas pour from his imagination through his fingers and his quill onto sheets of paper arrayed around his small room. The pages are collected, copied, studied and at some distant place, the premier of this symphony takes place, unheard by this man yet heard so perfectly within his head. Rapturous applause is also as distant from his experience as the notes and harmonies of the symphony, acclaim for another great work might percolate through the written record of the day.
This story, fanciful as it may be and loaded with the delivered imagery of Beethoven as some mad genius, contains several elements of truth and illuminates several problems and possibilities that a complete and useful notational system can offer. In this chapter we aim to investigate some of these things and see the ways in which these ideas interrelate.

Reading, Writing and Reception

The first way of looking at this fanciful anecdote is seeing the processes taking place. Music, symphonic and complex, emerges in the mind of a composer. How exactly this happens is probably one of the big questions of life and creativity, but we will have more to imagine about this later. For now let us suppose that it appears fully formed in his imaginative genius centre, problematic as that idea is. The first thing that happens is that a process of *writing* takes place. Using an existing notational system with possible side notes and other marks of meaning, the writer transfers the imagination of sound into a series of notes played by a number of instruments at various times, with speeds changing and dynamics building from melody to effect. This act of translation is perhaps one of the most mysterious.
The next process to take place is one of reading -the conductor, musicians and other associated people work through the score, imagining parts, practicing lines, deciding which instruments and how many thereof will be needed to turn this score into a performance. Maybe someone will change the page breaks to make the playing more straightforward in a performance scenario, another person will re-write on another staff as they come from a slightly different tradition. They will read, they will understand, they will adapt and enlarge, adding nuances or arguing over emphasis, the violins will rehearse and discuss the difficulties and the conductor will work out how to balance all the pieces into a whole. As the night of the premiere approaches, the details of coordination will come together, scribbled marginal notes will be

Thoughts on Notation

corrected and the form will become apparent.

On the night of the performance, a process of reception[1] takes place. The audience made of a huge spectrum of people, from fawning courtiers through to highly proficient musicians, will hear the piece as delivered by the orchestra. They will listen and enjoy, they will be transported by melodies or astounded by timpani, some will close their eyes and dream, others will focus on the prancing conductor and the sawing violins, full of enraged and active energy. Perhaps the conductor escapes his lonely deathbed room to sit and enjoy the spectacle, watching his music affect people so deeply, perhaps he will watch the musicians and follow his imagined sound of the symphony in his mind as it matches and differs from that which is delivered. A non-deaf composer might be able to annoy the conductor at rehearsals, our deaf old man can only gaze upon what he sees and attempt to bring imagination and its visual effects into alignment.

Legibility

The core action in this process is, to our minds, that of reading. One of the core properties of a notational system is that of readability. The *Voynich Manuscript* has been created by an apparently intelligent person or persons, it meets all the requirements of a text made of symbols to be formally nontrivial, yet no one knows of what it speaks. This text is unreadable, yet we believe that the notation it uses is that of a language that is meant to be telling us something. The rantings of seers and the insane, the scribbled pages of paranoid notes written in code, are also unintelligible. Thus we cannot speak of a notational in any useful sense of the word, unless there is, at least, the possibility of reading.

There is a story of a scientist, high on ether in the process of experiments in the 18th century, who reached an epiphany of total understanding late one night. Unable to recall the content of his epiphany the next morning, he resolved to undertake the same experiment but with a notebook in his hand, ready to document, notate or otherwise capture the essence that he had discovered. The experiment succeeded, contrary to what we would expect, epiphany was reached, and the next morning he read, in large letters, "Everything is brown."[2] Two immediate explanations arise. The first is that the epiphany was not as good as it seemed, as the understanding reached was somewhat less than enlightening. Another interpretation is that the way that his shamanic mind was working enabled a certain very compact summary of his epiphany and, if only he and we could understand the notation, the words, their positioning, the twists of their lines, all these things would convey the content of his experience. A third explanation might be that this attempt at a universal notation, able to explain the secrets of the universe and proffer a theory of everything, is a notational impossibility, and such dragons ought only be avoided unless one is well equipped, brave and in good company.

For now let us assume that notational systems in which we are interested are defined by a minimum level of readability. What does such readability require, what can help it, what might be a simple nice to have? On the most essential of levels, we need shared knowledge. An Australian Aboriginal meeting a well educated enlightenment scholar in Botany Bay in 1788 would find very little in common other than the shared experience of what they saw and that of being humans. Upon such commonalities much can be built, in particular language. In a notational system we want to assume much more, as a notational system should enable a shortening of description and the transmission of ideas and experiences. For this the writer and reader, or let us call them the users, of a given notated thing, have to agree on what they are talking about and how they will divide up the world. Skirting these issues of epistemology and all that jazz, a dragon lair of the most difficult sort, we talk blithely of a shared terminology as the ability to be speaking about the same things and to agree what words or other symbols to use to refer to these things. When an instrument builder and a composer talk of music, they will have difficulties as the instrument maker talks of timbre and resonances while the composer thinks in melodies and counterpoint. When discussing game experience, a player speaks of flow and being lost, a graphic designer of grittiness and distracting Moire effects.

Not only technical issues, but also cultural issues, the cultural context, plays a huge role. Writing three violin parts in the context of an orchestra means that there will be several violinists playing each of those parts, the existence of orchestras themselves are dependent upon so many element including the lack of amplification, the accumulation of wealth, management structures of orchestral discipline and the display of social importance.

Reproducibility

From a score, a notated piece of music, one also expects that the resulting readings give the same result (to the required level of "same") each time the piece is read. This begs the question of sameness, which is closely related to our levels of description, which turtle we are looking at. A Fluxus piece consisting of a short instruction "draw a straight line and follow it"[3] lives primarily from the openness of interpretation. We expect to recognise the reflected melodies in a performance of the *Goldberg Variations*, whether played on piano, harpsichord or ukelele. Every implementation of a schematic diagram should give a circuit that works in exactly the same way. The descriptive form of a folk music piece performed in a remote alpine village should contain enough information that an ethnomusicologist can identify similarities to related histories and see the changes that have happened in the ensuing years when she re-visits the village and hears the same piece passed on through generations since the original notating. Whether the description is a sound recording, a video, a description of the movements or an annotated score, all these might have some use. And they should hopefully enable if not the reproduction of the piece, then at least a comparison of the piece with another similar piece.

The idea that a composer should, based upon their previous experience with the ensembles for whom they write, be able to imagine the music very closely while writing a score, is a very strong idea of the role and capacity of a composer. This idea requires that the composer is working on a level that is deep enough that the resulting instance of that score being played is very close to their intention. Many of the examples we saw above allow a lot of freedom in the interpretation of the piece. These are written at a higher turtle than Beethoven did.

The determination of the audience plays a vital role in the selection of a notation. Who are the implementers of the description, what are their concepts, cultural contexts, levels of detail. We come here very quickly to questions of which turtles we need to be talking about. A stage director discussing a piece might discuss the music in terms of emotional changes and rhythmic strength when speaking to the head of music, but will talk about the length of a held note when talking directly to the musician during a rehearsal. Here we can get lost in our discussion of turtles and the determinism that our symbol systems enforce upon us and we refer to those chapters for those and related details. For readability questions we are concerned with the commonalities. The commonalities can be most quickly built up, explored and the missing commonalities repaired in a one to one dialogue. The *audience of one* scenario, where two people sit together to discuss a situation intensely, allows close read-write loops, discussing a situation with each person holding a pen in their hand, agreeing upon symbols and their use, the scope of the page its what it is staging changing as they discuss, reflect and reflexively build a notational system. Two people, tight reactive loops, a system that can react and grow quickly.

8. Beethoven's Deathbed

Taking this idea one step further, the *audience of zero* scenario leaves the reader, writer and creator of the notational system in one person, scribbling, drawing and trying to explain to themselves what it is that is going on in a given situation. Through the externality of a score one is confronted with one's own imagination and through attempts to understand what it means one can discover the faults in a structure, the strange curves of an argument, the open question at the end of a story. Not only is a dialogue with oneself through the externalised possible, but argument, banter and perhaps even heckling become part of the externalised internal monologue. Looking at a scribbled curve, drawing a circle around it and writing "HUH!?" to let yourself know that you do not know what you are talking about. Then starting to defend one's position or develop a refinement, building the piece through externalised introspection.

We could go further and claim that the externalised nature of notation, where a creator gets the ideas out of their head and drawn onto paper, chalked onto a blackboard, scratched in the dirt or summarised in some other notational form, is the creation of a new other. This other is a colleague with whom the creator can converse on equal terms, constructing the notation themselves, and thus get a grip on what they are trying to do and develop the piece iteratively. Whether sketches, doodles, snippets of text or music, diagrams of lights and their movements, all these forms allow a single creator to explore the possibilities of their ideas and thus create. Thus the idea introduced above, that the symphony appears fully-fledged in the mind of the genius, is most likely false. Snippets and ideas appear, are sketched, assembled, collected and re-worked until the notated piece, the score, can be looked at and the whole thing can be apprehended and thought about as a single thing. There is an argument that notation is one tool on the path to acts of so-called genius.

---

1. Reception as a generalised form of listening. This might be a wobbly concept. But it is probably a very wobbly concept and has been thought about by much cleverer people than us.
2. Other versions of the story have various other more or less meaningless statements including a smell of petroleum.
3. One of the "Compositions 1960" by La Monte Young (*1935-)

Thoughts on Notation

STEAL THIS NOTATION!

What do we need to think about in order to create notation? How might we consider the role of symbols and tools in building a notation system? For artists who use notation in their everyday work - electronic or otherwise - it is clear that every notation system has a specific aesthetic, whether we are aware of that or not. When we build scores in particular, from combined notation systems, it helps to be explicit about how tools and selections of symbols contribute to a specific aesthetic. This chapter is about creating new notation systems using the example of artistic practice. It is about how existing tools are influencing us in the process of creating new notation systems, and out of notation systems, scores.

For every notation system to become a meaningful system, there is a precondition of agreement on a common terminology in a specific cultural context. For instance in the practice of electronic music, there are terms like filter, envelope, curve, digit, line and Fast Fourier transform (FFT), where this specific community would have an understanding of what is being referred to, including the complexity of the terms themselves. In building a new notation system, you could use different symbols for these, but usually you are determined by already existing systems and tools.

Artists often find themselves in the position of creating new notation systems. The prospect of creating 'new' systems happens when you are dissatisfied with the utility of the systems you are using. But of course you are influenced by the systems you know, and out of that literacy, you are creating something new, from literacy in the old systems. You need to think: what do I want to describe and who do I want to address? We want to think about meaningful or useful symbols for this. These are key questions.

Symbols

Most used symbols in notation systems are visual. Examples of audible or gestural symbol do exist. Gestural symbols are used for example the person at the airport who helps the planes to come in with lit signs in his hands, or a realtime improvisational conductor, use gestural symbols. Morse code (as well as being visual) is an audible example. Any kind of sonic warning sign exists in an intelligible social system of sounds (such as a shark alarm in a beach town, versus a fire alarm). Audible notation can also take place in a musical score in which players get audio instructions via headphones, for example.

Parameters

The term parameter, connected with disciplines like maths, logic, linguistics and environmental science, came into play in art in the 1950s, with the emergence and artistic use of tools allowing practitioners to actually measure functions like frequency, amplitude and so on. Any function's properties and their transition from one state to another will be expressed with the values of a specific parameter space. In digital tools the parameter space for amplitude is commonly defined to be between 0.0 and 1.0. All values in between are possible measurements of this parameter, so 0.0 is silence and 1.0 is the maximum value without distortion.

The next examples show the selection of different symbols for envelope in sound and music analysis. An envelope is the enclosing "shape" of a sound. The basic parameters of an envelope are time and amplitude. The envelope is the way that amplitude varies over time. For example, the envelope of an organ is constant 1.0 from the moment that the key is pressed until it is released, where the amplitude abruptly falls to zero. The envelope of a piano with no pedal starts at 1.0 when the key is pressed, fades exponentially as the key is held, then abruptly falls to zero when the key is released. If the pedal is held, the exponential fade continues even when the key is released. A bowed string instrument such as a violin can have a more complex envelope as the bowing action allows the amplitude of a sound to be raised and lowered as the note or melody is played.

The notation symbols chosen for an envelope can vary. In the first example, we choose a graph and a curve as a graphic expression showing the values of the parameters: amplitude and time. As time goes on, the curve describes the amplitude of sound that the instrument creates. The curve moves up to represent larger amplitude, the horizontal axis represents zero amplitude.

A curve described graphically.

In the second example of the same envelope, we can choose digits to represent the same values with the same parameters. At time 0.0, I have an ampliturde of 0.0. At time 2.3, I have an amplitude of 0.3 and so on. This is notated a series of pairs of numbers, the first being the time, the second being the amplitude. The series is arranged with time values increasing to indicate the process of amplitude over time to create the envelope.
0.0 0.0, 2.3 0.3, 4.6 0.2, 5.4 0.28, ...
Such a notation is of less value for a human instrumentalist, but is useful for a mechanical or computational system. It can also be used for analysis procedures or the development of accompaniment. A piece of music could be described by a collection of parameters over time, amplitudes and frequencies, acoustic density and placement of sounds between various speakers. The paramenters might be musically very explicit auch as notes, or more general in terms of aggressivity, distortion, tension and volume.

Tools Determinism

The tools we are working with influence the selection and aesthetics of symbols that we choose to create. At the same time, a tool could already have a set of symbols embedded in it, for example a program like *Pure Data* (PD) (or similarly VVVV or Max/MSP, visual dataflow languages in general; we will use PD as our example) has a symbol for objects, messages, number boxes and so on. Furthermore, these symbols already have quite a complex meaning. So there is a difference between kinds of tools - a tool like PD having existing symbols with complex meaning, or a tool like a pencil.

In programs used to create electronic art, we are used to having a number of different boxes connected to each other on our screen. This is not just a function of PD but it also has a long pre-history of cabling and devices, or more generally processes and data flow, impacting upon the thinking and aesthetics of these notation systems in general. Such images, coming from the tool, will influence our approach to create notation systems and scores. And with that, the aesthetics of the system and the work being produced. We will think in terms of data inputs causing changes and resulting outputs, a "data push" metaphor, such as a knob turn causing frequency change in a sound or colour change in a screen object. It is worth mentioning that screen-output based systems such as VVVV can be optionally viewed as "data pull" systems where each video frame pulls down data, ignoring the data that arrives between frames to set the colour of a screen object with the newest input data value. Here the notational system is the same but

Thoughts on Notation

there are subtle and possibly very important changes in the way that the notated system works.

In the following example, a notation for electronic instruments written on paper is influenced by the aesthetics of PD. Here we are influenced to think in terms of streams of data, whether it be parameter values, sound or video, flowing between boxes that manipulate, store and pass on those streams.

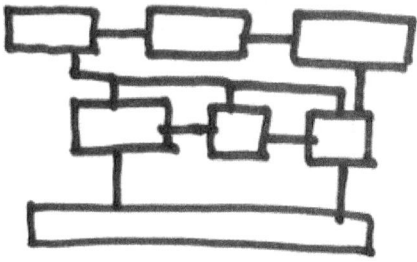

Data flow description of modular sound system.

Many practitioners could imagine a selection of ways that this particular arrangement could make sense, and with some internal notation about the function of each box, this could work as a notation for a computer music system. It might also be used to describe an analogue synthesizer or an analogue video effects system.

If your tool is a guitar, you might be drawing on a notation system such as the following, where the immediate influence is to think of chords and harmony.

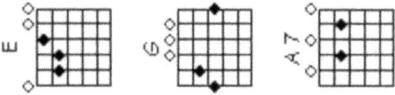

Three chords for guitar described graphically.

Notating chord based guitar music can be done by using these symbols arranged appropriately over the page, for instance at appropriate points adjacent to the text of a song, or replacing them with the abbreviations describing the chord (E, G, A7). Rather than the more explicit description of the position of the fingers, we could simply write A7 to mean the A seventh chord. These two notations would be equivalent in terms of their informational content, where one reminds the reader of the hand shape of the chord, while the second relies on a level of

9. Steal This Notation!

expertise.

Such a series of symbols, whether chord names or chord diagrams, is however of little use in a PD environment, and a guitarist would have trouble thinking how to play the data flow description above if not in posession of a large number of effects devices.

Symbols and Levels of Abstraction

A specific symbol is not necessarily connected to a specific level of abstraction (or turtle) within a notation system. In fact there is no necessity to connect a specific symbol to a specific layer of abstraction. But in many cases it turns out that some specific symbols are more relevant than others, depending upon the specific level of abstraction.

On a higher level, one might choose a spoken language to describe what one wants. For example, in the notation "Play a Melody", everything is open except that it's a melody. There are many refinements possible without leaving the realm of natural language. "Play a joyous melody" or "Play a familar melody slightly wrongly" lead somewhere, "Play a melody and repeat it until it breaks" leads somewhere else entirely. "Play a melody and follow it" references a Fluxus tradition which brings in a whole swathe of other possibly important implications, not mentioned in the notation itself.

The following is a different level of abstraction: on the one hand it's less abstract but it's not getting rid of a large degree of openness.

A musical staff with three notes indicating pitch and duration.

In this notation much more is defined - the rhythm, tonality - but what is totally open is who or what is playing it, so it also is extremely open. The rhythm is there but not the meter, there is no indication of instruments. However the use of modern Western staff notation would indicate a certain cultural milieu, the non-use of printed parallel lines adds a certain casual approach which might lead to a more effusive and frivolous playing style.

In any one notation system you can have different layers of abstraction and combine them. It is the combination that is specific to a particular outcome. For example, you might want to be really detailed about the timing of a note, but you also might just want to say, regarding the volume, "play it really loud." A high level of abstraction for one symbol might be leaving things open for interpretation, but this is totally context dependent (very abstract symbols can mean very specific things to specialist communities of practice).

It is also the case that the same notation, interpreted by different interpreter communities or practitioners, can change the level of abstraction without changing the symbols. For example, let's say I have a video in which a person is moving from A to B. Let's give this video as a score to a musician for musical interpretation. In this case, you have a high level of abstraction in the score. The musician has a wide range of interpretation possibilities, yet there is a certain notational consistency with time, rhythm and other actors. If you use the same video as a score for a human performer, who you want to do a very similar traversal – from a point A to point B in a similar space of performance as the original score, then in this second instance and use of this score, the notation is very precise and laborious that it becomes fairly useless as a notation for further performances other than replications of the original.

Scores

With tools, symbols and parameters, artists create a score. There are at least two different kind of scores. There are scores meant for interpretation, which are always an algorithm, such as a recipe, which aims to be put into action by an interpreter. The second kind of score's purpose is to make a transcription or documentation of an action that has taken place already. In this part we are talking only about scores for interpretation.

In order to escape the uniqueness of a performance or instatiation, we might wish to require that the symbols in a score should have the potential to be executed by any suitable software with any hardware, by any human being able to connect to the context. Chosen symbols for a score should go beyond a specific software or hardware creating a metalanguage for interpretation. The main purpose is to leave a structure which has the potential to be transferred to other systems. This means that our score should lie above the level of structural isomorphism with the resulting music.

The following is a piece of Arduino code, relevant only for a specific environment. It is not fulfilling the requirements of a score, as it is isomorphic to the process that it encodes and notates.

```
s->selectBank ( BANK_A );
```

9. Steal This Notation!

```
s->setPatch ( OSC_1_TO_MIXER | OSC_2_TO_MIXER | OSC_3_TO_MIXER);
s->setWaveform ( OSC_ALL, SINE);
s->setFrequency ( OSC_1 , 40.0f);
s->setFrequency ( OSC_2, 77.0f);
s->setFrequency ( OSC_3, 1.9f);
s->setAmplitude ( OSC_1, 0.2f );
s->setAmplitude ( OSC_2, 0.3f );
s->setAmplitude ( OSC_3, 0.4f );
```

This next example of a notation, with the same meaning as the example above, is open to many possible systems and interpreters and therefore could be executed by any machine and any human being. If you know the terminology, the diagram is fulfilling the requirements of a score. In this case its up to the interpreter which kind of oscillating system being used: an electronic oscillator, a string, a voice, motorised devices, three tractors, etc.

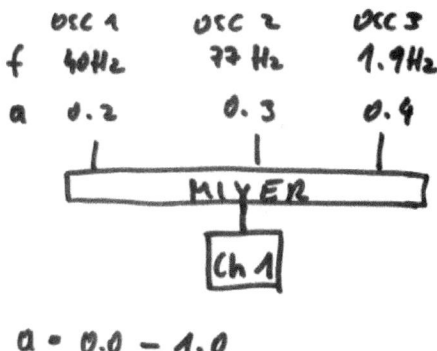

A diagram of three oscillators being fed to a mixer and a single channel sound system.

Mixing Systems and Symbols to create Scores

When we make a score we can express the same instructions in different ways, choosing symbols from different notation systems and combining them. We can combine different notation systems and use different levels of abstractions. There are no rules and no limits. We have said that a notation system or language has specific rules (grammar) and a limited set of symbols (alphabet). We might regard the notation system of a score as the union or collection of the used notational systems, in order to be formal.
Consider the same algorithm/score expressed in different ways:
1.) move from A to B

Thoughts on Notation

This notation system is a subset of the English language (sentence).
The symbols are Latin letters A and B, and the words "move", "from", "to". The grammar or inner logic of the notational system seems to allow sentences of the form "move x to y" where x and y can be a capital letter.

2.) A → B

The notation system is a subset of the English language, but it is combined with symbols of arrows.
The symbols are Latin letters and arrows. The grammar might be "x → y" where x and y can be any capital letter. This might feel a bit mathamatical, or like a football coach talking about movements across the playing field.

3.) A$^\Phi$B

The notation systems are subsets of the English and Greek language.
The symbols are Latin and Greek letters and the system is otherwise the same as the version with arrows. This system derives more strongly from a history of linear algebra describing certains types of processes of transformation from a structure A to a structure B.

4.)

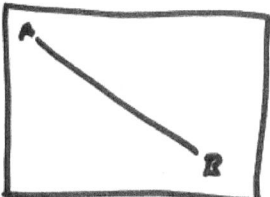

The notation system is graphics and a subset of the English language.

The symbols are straight lines, and Latin letters. The grammar might be that the symbol must be a rectangle, two capital letters are within the rectangle and the two capital letters are joined by a straight line.

Some of these notational systems are isomorphic, some are more specific. We would claim that the first three systems are equivalent, while the fourth example contains position information and is thus more specific.

This is an example of a score with mixed symbols from different notation systems:

9. Steal This Notation!

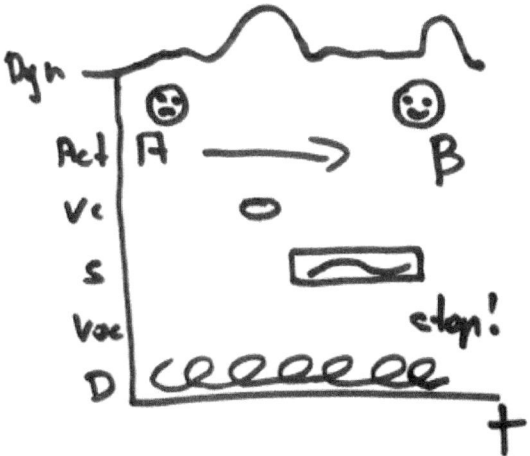

dyn= dynamic, Act=actor, Vc=violoncello,

S=sinewave, Voc=vocals, D=dancer, t=time

A complete score describing a performance piece for three musicians, an actor and a dancer.

With a score like this, very common in contemporary art practice, the interpreters are forced to use their imagination based in their specific cultural context. Questions will arise like: How long, with which pitch and timbre should the whole note be played? What kind of movement will the dancer choose? How will all the interpreters coordinate themselves?

Is this mix a new notation system or is it a score using mixed symbols from different existing notation systems? It depends. If it was used just for one score, then arguably it is not a new notation system, but it could be a starting point for the creation of a new notation system with rules, a limited vocabulary and set of symbols, and a developing inner logic. Here we are at a point, where we may indeed recognize the creation of a new notation system.

Thoughts on Notation

IT'S THE CULTURAL CONTEXT, SCHTOOPID!

It is a banality but ever worth saying, that the context of any utterance is needed to comprehend that utterance. Some statements require less immediate context, such as Pythagoras' Theorem, whereas the statement "I completely agree except about the birds" is unintelligible. And nothing less can be said about notations. Every notation lies in its context, with an intention, a purpose, assumptions and presumptions.

When a young person says "wimp" they are probably referring to some weakness of the object of derision. When a physicist says wimp she says it with capital letters and a WIMP is a Weakly Interacting Massive Particle. This in turn means that they are speaking of a subatomic particle with mass (so not e.g. a photon) that experiences the weak force but not the strong or electromagnetic forces as well as the gravitational force and are a possible explanation for so called "dark matter." Jargon is a form of notation, the use of the word WIMP precludes the necessity to explain a whole broad swathe of concepts.

So jargon is a shorthand. Jargon also creates communities, people who can use that jargon clump together and become a self selecting group, a localised cultural context. With this existing shorthand, verbal communication is accelerated. A similar role is played by the creation of notations - finding a symbol for a concept enables that concept to be easily manipulated.

This brings us to our turtles once again - choosing the right level of expression has to do with the cultural context into which one is creating a score. The level of detail should not be mind numbingly high, with precise movements sending all to sleep but the technicians, nor too low, when it will be greeted as a form of handwaving.

A given community also chooses the types of things they want to do with a notational system, formulating types of questions and ways of asking. This thus informs the types of things that the notational system will be asked to do. A group of improvising electronic musicians have little use for a notation system for melodies, but might have a strong desire to form a notation to define the way that each musician can take and modify the performance of another. An improvising theatre group cares not about the words of a piece but the structure of how they can build a piece from the three words given by the audience - a well composed piece allows them and even forces them to develop an entrancing story by forcing them into certain structures within which they can find the needed dialogue and movement for their characters as they develop them.

The type of explanations that we are content with depend upon the culture within which we live. In a modern urban scientific-technological society, a storm is explained and written with a synoptic chart and a summary of air movements, we see it coming with a fall in barometric pressure. An animist society will foresee the storm by observing ants' movements and where birds are flying and might explain it with the moods of gods and spirits unhappy with the way the community is acting.

A community does activities and undertakes projects. By taking things that exist and working out ways of summarising them, we work out what our practice is and that form of compactification leads to simplifications. Those simplifications are a form of notation, inasmuch we have ways of speaking about them that other people understand. Depending upon the activities that we undertake, certain forms of notating become more amenable and usable. Through the spread of computers, the business technique of using spreadsheets has spread as a cultural technique so that people are more happy about creating things in a spreadsheet environment and can understand that type of information display. The idea of using boxes and arrows to describe processes or hierarchical relationships has also become a widespread technique and forms of notation that use this, such as *LabView* for designing laboratory data acquisition and manipulation or *Pure Data* for sound and data manipulation, income inequalities or complex arrays of company ownership as diagrammed in *TheyRule*, have become relatively easily understood.

The audience remains an important issue in interactive art pieces. Who are they? In many cultural productions there are two audiences that are apparent. One is the audience who will use the end product of the production. The requirements for a serious game and those for a children's game are widely different and will greatly effect what is in the production. However the audience that is perhaps most relevant for notation is not the user audience but the people who are helping create the piece - programmers, designers, etc. The notation used to communicate within the team producing a piece will be dependent upon all the things that that team have done and the way that they can work together, experiences with various forms of communication and their understanding of what their role can be. Beside that this team has to notate instructions for the user audience and even more, to make a record of the users' interaction behaviour that will be relevant for further strategies and might lead into considerations for specific cultural context adaptions.

Interactivity

WHAT IS INTERACTIVITY?

So far we have been talking about actions and the notation for actions. What happens, in what order, when in relation to what else. We see actions, people, systems, machines acting in the world. Taking Maturana's ideas of autopoietic systems, one is confronted with the idea of borders of systems and the allowable effects across those borders. This surface, we could call an interface. The idea of interactive systems, as opposed to active and reactive systems, has to do with a looping series of actions and reactions between two or more actors.

Ah, this sounds so easy!

A Note to Academics

This discussion about what interactivity is could, has and will continue to fill volumes. As doctorates are written, as artworks and business models are planned and made, as people act, react and interact, as all this happens people will continue to think about the fundamental nature of interactivity, what it means, what it does, why we do it, what the point might be. In this miasma we dare not tread or dive any deeper than absolutely necessary, thus we would like to suggest a simple, a naive yet hopefully not too wrong concept of interfaces, interactivity and all the conundrums associated with it.

One of the silliest yet most telling typographical errors as we write such words is the introduction of the term *interreactive*. While unintended, this expression seems fortuitous. When we talk of interaction, we really are talking about inter-reaction.

Let us appraoch this with an example.

At the first level, we have action. I walk to the corner. The next level is reaction. I insert some money in a vending machine and press a button, some chocolate comes out. The machine has reacted to me, but I have not, in any useful sense, reacted to the machine. I see a friend, I say hello, they reply, I offer some chocolate, we converse about the day, we decide to go for a drink, a long night ensues. This is interaction of the finest sort. If my friend did not react to my actions by realising I needed a good talk, if I did not react to my friend by realising she was hungry and needed dinner, then our mutual understandings would be shallower, our friendship would be less deep.

We would like to claim that the typo has given us a new idea, that we are interested in interreaction, but will succumb to popular usage and stick with interaction, at least for now.

Interactivity

How to Recognise it in the Wild

So what are some of the properties of this interactivity thing? While the feedback loops must exist, they need not be realtime. A game of chess is interactive, the board acting as an interface between the players. The game can be so slow as to be played by mail, with days passing between moves. Much mail art might also fall ino this category, with musicians exchanging tapes that they use to build upon and create new versions, remixes and other modifications before sending on a tape of the updated piece. We would not hesitate to call this an interactive process. However in many cases simultaneity is necessary, whether the interaction is arm wrestling or improvised music. Arm wrestling with even a small delay could prove tragically impossible or even dangerous. Improvised music most often lives from the realtime liveness of the experience, as the musicians bounce off one another, come together and create something through rhythmic, tonal and physical proximity.

Here we see an example of where multiple actors in a network have different experiences of an interactive moment. A good conductor responds to the orchestra and the nuances of their playing as they respond to her movements and guides, an interactive moment of interest for a number of reasons. However the third actor in this network, the audience member, has no significant effect upon the orchestra or the conductor, only able to listen. The act of listening can be active, with the listener actively participating, but there is no clear effect back to the orchestra-conductor unit to let a truly interactive moment occur. On the other hand in a small venue, two musicians playing together will be interacting strongly as they play together, the audience will respond to their music and the reactions of the audience, illuminated by the lights spilling offstage, will effect the musicians once again forming a multisided network of interactivity.

With all likelihood there are a swathe of connections to sender-receiver theory, actor-network theory and a whole bunch of other well-thought-out philosophical, sociological and psychoneurological theories and studies to undermine, support, contradict or twist these ideas in a number of ways. Inasmuch as we are not too wrong, we will leave these things by the roadside, comment upon them as interesting but not for now, and carry on with our plan to have a working idea of interaction.

Experthood and Nesting

We think it is worthwhile to introduce one more idea about interaction that we have found useful, that of nested interactivity. This has been mentioned above in the discussion about orchestras, conductors and audiences, but we think there is a better description worth thinking about.

When we first start to move, according to many theories of very early childhood development, our perceptual systems and motor systems are pretty messy, unstructured and chaotic, even random. As the flush of sensory information falls upon our skin, eyes, ears and other sensory systems, we begin to organise, arrange and understand how this all fits together. This seems to be some deep fundamental human property, whether or not we are a blank slate at birth. Our eyes develop the ability to recognise shapes, then we begin to register the actions of our hands and feet. Anecdotal evidence of the surprise and joy on a child's face as they work out the connection between certain muscle actions and the resulting hand actions indicate that there is a part of our lives when we are learning to even use our hands, taking advantage of feedback. Tension a muscle, watch the movement of a limb, recognise a gesture. We see this in the more tragic case of people who have lost the use of certain nerves, brain regions or body parts and who are painfully re-learning to use their bodies using all sorts of feedback loops.

But at some point, with luck, it becomes sublimated and the act of grasping is natural, reaching out, holding things, moving and placing are all second nature actions that no longer consciously use the feedback loops involved. Our mind is free to do more interesting things like learn to talk, throw toys around in order to experiment with gravity and other such basic science.

When we receive an instrument the first time, say a violin, the scratchy sound that is produced is a horror to the ears. As we play a bit, trying things out, we tense muscles, changing pressure upon the strings, the angle of the bow, the speed of movement. A tight feedback loop is created between the motions of our hands, the effects upon the fiddle, the reactions as sound and our reactions to that sound as we try to correct our actions to make the sound less horrifying. This learning process goes on and as we move forward, we begin to sublimate the feedback loops so that the sound of the bow across the strings is not modulated by the errors in our presssure correction loop but by our desire to have a sound that modulates the intensity of its sound, the bite of the notes, the abruptness of the staccato attacks. Our fingers on the fingerboard wobble not to find the note but because we are modulating it ever so slightly to add a tragic vibrato. At this point, our conscious mind has to focus less on the feedback interaction loop of the violin and our hands and we are freed up to pay attention to the conductor of the ensemble, to wink at handsome men walking past on

Interactivity

the street as they toss a donation or listen to our colleagues and improvise freely without too much technical distraction.

Reacting Reactors - *HMO*

Rocket scientists might at times be helpful but are not of essential importance to having a working interactive system. In fact the minimum requirements to be met by an entity are very very basic. Being able to react to a stimulus is all that is needed to start playing the game of interactivity. When analysing some simple interactive systems the entities acting and re-acting within these systems with one and another can be divided into three major groups:
Humans (H): this group is rather self explanatory
Machines (M): For the purpose at hand, "machine" will describe any human-made device able to react to a stimulus, thus being able to be a reacting entity in an interactive system.
Other (O): "Other" is an umbrella term for any entity which is neither human nor machine and able to react to a stimulus. This group contains also but is not limited to animals, plants, and aliens (once they visit). It is not just "objects" at all!
There are several possible one-on-one scenarios for interaction as all interaction is happening via a channel or media (think telephone/computer interface and the like).

Human-human - *HH*

This being the most common form of interaction and probably also the richest in terms of complexity and occurence is left out without being a dragon in itself but simply because of the enormous scope of the field

11. What is Interactivity?

which is covered to great extent elsewhere, from psychology to novels. It will however be on the radar if it occurs within the boundaries of a formal interactive system. There are complex analysis techniques used to notate human language and human conversations, which may be of value to plunder for inspiration.

Machine-machine - *MM*

Machines "talking" to one and another is also a rather common, but mostly ignored event. One just has to think of mail servers communicating and actually having a dialogue via a protocol with a connected computer running an email program.

The protocol for such an interaction on the internet is well defined with RFCs (Requests For Comments, the standards of the internet) describing the various parts of the protocol. These RFCs set up a notation to describe the actions and reactions of each agent in such a MM interaction, this formal description of the protocol allows an analysis of the process in order to confirm that the protocol is error free. It is also possible to verify any given server implementation against the protocol, in essence to confirm that the particular implementation, the code, does no more and no less than that which is required by the notation in the RFC. This formality is a great strength of MM interactions, there are many notations available to specify, analyse and implement various parts of the MM interaction. This is used in the practicalities of programming environments where the validity of machine state can be tested, formal tests such as *lint* for the C programming language and the various web standard testers to ensure that web code abides by the structured of the HTML standard.

Interactivity

Note that while there is a strong formalism for these interactions, there are other standards which are brought to bear. Postel's Law, whih dates from the implementation of TCP, states that an "implementations should follow a general principle of robustness: be conservative in what you do, be liberal in what you accept from others." While it can be argued that this resilience allows inferior implementations to survive, and is thus problematic, the usefulness of it will probably continue to overwhelm the possible negatives.

Other-other - *OO*

Dogs chasing cats and cats ignoring dogs shows that interactivity is in no way dependent on the inclusion of humans or machines. Trying to work out what is going on is the work of horse whisperers and ethologists, shepherds and cognitive scientists. It is unlikely that we can use any formalisms of machine based interactions or the introspection of humans to gain insight into what is really going on.

Human-machine - *HM*

Many hours of potentially productive human lifetime are invested in this kind of interactivity (think Pong, think DOOM). Human-machine interaction happens via an interface and (in most cases) beholds the necessity of a translation process between the entities. HM is often a cover for the more complex HMH where machines interleave and make HH interactions possible. Whether this is the social software of Web 2.0 or the social hardware of shared interactive installations makes no real difference.

The HM relationship is the one most amenable and interesting to analyse, as we can borrow from the formality of MM and the introspection of HH. It is also the place where a lot of the interesting things happen. Given human introspection and the formality of machine actions, we can and do build examples of the formalisms of these interactions.

Human-other - *HO*

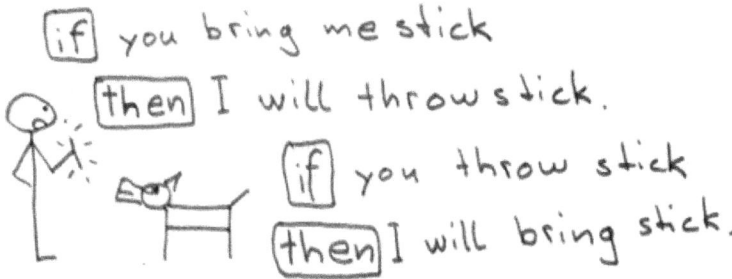

Everyone ever having thrown a stick to be returned by a playful dog has experienced the joy lying in the repetitive interaction with something not being a machine or a human. As the above example shows so well "if" and "then" are essential to interactivity. Changes in actions must lead to changes in consequences.

Unable to ascribe too much to an O entity, we are in an interesting position of analysis. As the example shows, we can attempt to analyse the interaction in a variety of pseudo code, notating the core elements of the interaction as intertangled if-then statements. If this described an MM interaction with its unwavering formaliy, then the two Ms would happily carry on throwing and bringing as long as the stick lasted. The replacement of Ms by an H and an O introduces a number of other possibilities including boredom, distraction and losing the stick up a tree.

Whether this can be notated meaningfully is yet another question.

Interactivity

Machine-other - *MO*

Thanks to behavioural science and its scientists, animals (even farm animals) also get to take IQ and other tests via touchscreens and other animal-computer interfaces. There is probably research money in this stuff, let's get to it.

This spectrum of basic interactions is merely a starting point. Interactive systems usually are composed of more than that minimum of two entities, giving social dynamics room to take effect and giving the participating entities the option to switch between being part of an interaction to just being an audience with limited or no influence on the path of events unfolding.

Wanting to be an Actor

The main focus will be laid on HM interactivity within a formal system, but the findings usually are valid for other variants of HMO interactions. The driving motivations for an entity to interact with another one within an interactive system are manifold, but some core motivations can be found far more frequently than others.
At a very general level the most potent motivator is joy. The methods of achieving the experience of joy may vary, but they all have in common that they make the individual want to continue or repeat the action that has led to this desirable condition. In (interactive) games it is often some form of success, a sense of achievement which keeps the actor "hooked" and wanting more. This search for joy via success in solving problems seems fundamental to (human) nature and even if initially it was curiosity or simple obedience to orders which put the individual in that problematic situation, the joy coming with success (even if received bit by bit in small doses) soon becomes the main drive for continuation

and repetition. At a first glance, the Stockholm Syndrome seems irrelevant for HM interaction, but perhaps it is not.

The main question for motivations is one of access, the first usage. What is the motivation to start an interactive experience? In the arts this is often less important as the piece will be presented in a space that self-selects people interested in exploring the possibility for interactive art. The question as to the welcoming nature of the interface and whether it is open and clear enough can be raised. I may be interested in interacting, but if I cannot see what the sensor might be or recognise any effects of my actions (i.e. the reaction is missing) then the initial action-reaction cycle has already gone wrong.

Hidden Layers

There is a large and interesting issue of visible, hidden and deeper levels of interaction. As we begin interacting with a system, it is often important to have clear reactions. As we begin to understand these interactions, our control of the interaction leads us to attempt finer control and, with a system of interest, we begin to dig deeper into the possibilities of the system. Initially these deeper levels might have been invisible because the sensors were not active or, more likely, the details of our actions were not subtle enough to evoke the deeper levels, somewhat like the first stages of learning the violin. The details of our actions were being observed by the system but the nuances were not comprehensible to us. The somewhat malicious version of this is the hidden interaction, where our interactions work according to our expectations, clicking a link and moving to a new page, but the extra interactions with a Google databank and thereon to the advertising world are hidden from view yet subtly apparent in the advertisements we are confronted with.

In the next two chapters we will be investigating certain systems and the possibilities to notate them in different ways. Since the path is dark and full of dangers, we won't attack any of the many complex and interesting platforms that most excite our imagination. Instead, we will follow the strategy of the common neuroscientist, who prefers to work with the humblest of creatures, the slug, in order to advance without missteps in a simpler researching enviroment. We will start from the earliest and simplest stars of the game world: the most beloved puzzle in history and the first computer game that ever was.

Enter Slug n°.1 and Slug n°.2.

Interactivity

SLUG Nº. 1: NOTATING THE RUBIK'S CUBE

Everybody knows the Rubik's Cube, a simultaneously frustrating and delightful 3D puzzle that is as iconic of an 80's childhood as Karate Kid and giant shoulder pads. Its creator, the Hungarian architect and designer Ernő Rubik, called it *Bűvös Kocka* (the Magic Cube) and it became so massively successful it even caused an impact on Hungary's economy (for the better). "The device is also sometimes called the Hungarian Horror" informed Time magazine on their March issue for 1981 "since it can induce temporary dementia in otherwise balanced citizens." Luckily for all of them, a bearded professor of mathematics created a notation system for it. So they could cheat.

The game was in fact an accident. Ernő was trying to resolve a problem for the class he was teaching at the Academy of Applied arts and Design: how blocks could move independently *without falling apart*. After several failed attempts involving elastic bands, he carved a wooden model where blocks were holding themselves together through a complex combination of position and shape and painted each side with a different color, as a breadcrumbs guide. It was when he tried to return the blocks to their original positions that The Magic was born.

> *It was wonderful to see how, after only a few turns, the colors became mixed, apparently in random fashion. It was tremendously satisfying to watch this color parade. Like after a nice walk when you have seen many lovely sites you decide to go home, after a while I decided it was time to go home, let us put the cubes back in order. And it was at that moment that I came face to face with the Big Challenge: What is the way home?*
>
> *Erno Rubik*

It took Rubik several weeks and numerous calculations to regroup the colors, but very little to understand the potential of his discovery: he applied for the Hungarian patent in January 1975. The Rubik's craze that followed resulted in many cheat books and newspaper pages of "easy" methods for resolving the puzzle, all using idiosyncratic notations with pitiful levels of usability. "Notes on Rubik's Magic Cube," published in 1980, introduced a method so simple and intuitive enough that would rapidly become the standard: the Singmaster's Notation.

David Singmaster was interested in Group Theory, a branch of abstract algebra where the focus of research is on structures more than numbers. His notation relies heavily on the position of the player, who must be looking at the cube from slightly above and to the right of it, from where he can see the three faces at the top, front and right.

Interactivity

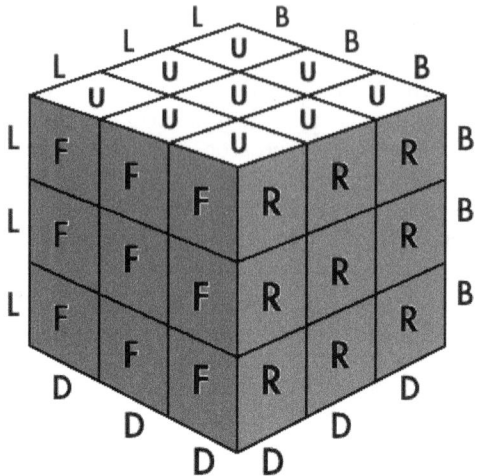

In the Singmaster notation, those faces are named "Up", "Front" and "Right" (U, F and R). The faces the player doesn't see, the bottom, back and left of the cube, are "Down", "Back" and "Left" (D, B and L).

- U for the Upper face
- F for the Front face
- D for the Down face
- B for the Back face
- L for the Left face
- R for the Right face

The Singmaster in Detail

A *score* in this notation is a series of moves which are defined as follows. A letter by itself indicates a quarter-turn clockwise. A prime symbol ['] after a letter means to turn the face counter-clockwise a quarter-turn. A letter followed by the numeral 2 (occasionally superscript) means to turn the face 180° (and it doesn't indicate direction because both clockwise and anticlockwise lead to the same place).
Changing to lowercase (*u, f, d, b, l and r*) indicates that the first *two* layers of that face must be twisted, leaving the third layer behind. This could of course be done in two movements but such is the ambition of the notation: to reduce the score to the minimum number of lines.
The inner layer of the cube has *Middle*, *Equatorial*, and *Side*, where *M* is turning the layer between *L* and *R* downward (clockwise if looking from the left side); *E* means turning the layer between *U* and *D* to the right

12. Slug n°. 1: Notating the Rubik's Cube

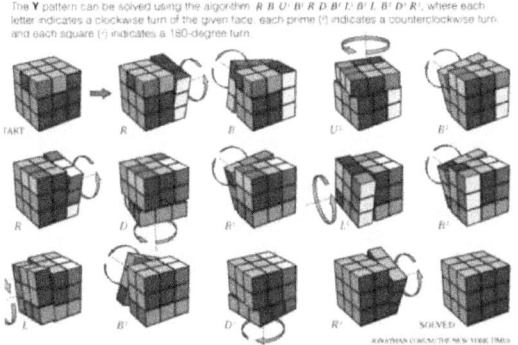

A sample of the popular CFOP or Fridrich Method

(counter-clockwise if looking from the top) and *S* means turning the layer between *F* and *B* clockwise.

When the whole cube must be turned about one of its axes, the notation prescribes a conventional axis indicators *X*, *Y*, and *Z*, where X is from left to right, Y from up to down and Z, from the front face to the back, but the rule is scarcely followed, since most players wisely prefer to say: turn the cube upside down.

Notating is Engineering, not Designing

Singmaster's solution allows for players to use "algorithms", which in the Rubik's universe is a sequence of moves that leads to the desired position. The *CFOP* method, more popularly but somehow controversially known as the *Fridrich Method*, requires that we first solve the first two layers. This is how the early cheatsheets or algorithms looked:

```
FR: (R U' R') Dw (R' U2) (R U'2) (R' U R)
FL: (L' U L Dw') (L U'2) (L' Dw2) (R U' R')
BR: (R' U R Dw') (R U2) (R' U'2) (R U' R')
BL: (L U'L' Dw) (L' U'2) (L U2) (L' U L)
```

What we learn is that a notation for a game must derive from its mechanics and not from its parts. The cube has 54 colored squares but, while that is precisely correct, it is not relevant, because not all of them can be rotated or rearranged. There are only 26 "cubies" that rotate on a central axis, of which 8 are corners, 12 edges, and 6 centers. Only 20 of them move, because the centers are fixed. The colors are, in this sense, also distracting for they do not group similar objects. The notation we have shown above is an action notation, it described how to manipulate the cube. It does not describe the state of the cube, the pattern of which cubies are in which position and orientation. The state of a given cube can be described by the cubie in each position and its orientation, written as a list. There are 8 corner cubies which can be in 3 different orientations, 12 edge cubies which can be in 2 different orientations, so 8+12=20 entries suffice to describe each cube state. This gives us a notation to describe states and thus count them, giving us $8!.3^8.12!.2^{12}$ =519,024,039,293,878,272,000 possible states.

The action notation of Singmaster introduced above allows us to move from one cube state to another. We have a state notation and an action notation.

The "Laws of a Rubik's Cube" matter greatly to the syntax. Following these coordinates, the cube can be oriented 24 ways: the upper face (U) can be selected in 6 different ways and, for each upper face, the front face can be selected in 4 different ways (6 × 4 = 24). Not every possible configuration of the cubies is possible. The player can only flip an even amount of edges and never twist 1,2,4,5,7 or 8 corners in the same direction. We can only cycle an odd number of pieces. If we found ourselves with only two pieces to swap, a single edge to flip or a single corner to twist, our cube is simply broken, or badly assembled, and cannot be resolved. It can be shown that there are 12 distinct collections of states of the cube, that no move will be able to take a cube in one collection to another collection. One of these collections includes the solved cube. If we find an odd number of swaps or a single corner is flipped, we know we are in one of the other state collections and cannot solve the cube. We thus also know that the number of states given above is too large by a factor of 12, but that does not make the number much easier to grasp.

A Curiosity: God's Number

Every serious player's ambition is perfection. In Go, a match between masters where every move is the best and most inspired possible is called divine *(Kami-no-Itte)*; in chess, a mistake-free match is casually known as *The Gold*. For speedcubers, there is God's number.

Speedcubers are the sports champions of cube solving. Given a cube in a random state, they endeavour to solve the cube as quickly as possible, either as a show of talent or in competition with other speedcubers. While fast fingers, well-lubricated cubes and muscle memory are important for fast solving, have a system with a very low number of

12. Slug nº. 1: Notating the Rubik's Cube

moves to solve a given cube state is probably the most important.

We say that the number of steps needed to solve the cube in a given state as the *distance* of that state from solved. Suppose that every state of the cube was a mark on the ground with a line between them if a move took you from one state to another. Then the distance of a given state is the lowest number of lines you would have to follow to move from that state along the lines.

There is only one state with distance zero, the solved state. We saw above that there are three different moves to be performed on each face, a clockwise turn, an anticlockwise turn and a 180° turn. Thus for each of six faces there are three moves to be performed, giving us 18 states at distance one. Calculating the number of states at larger distances is harder.

The following question arises for speedcubers: what the furthest distance any position can be from solved? What is the smallest number such that every state of a cube can be solved in that number of steps or less? This is called God's Number.

In 1995 Michael Read showed that the *superflip* position, a nastily symmetric state of the cube, requires 20 moves to solve. There is no shorter sequence of moves. Thus it was known that God's Number was at least 20. Researchers had a lower bound for God's Number, perhaps there is a state that requires even more moves. Since July 2010, thanks to Google's computational donation equivalant to 35 CPU years of desktop computer power, we know that no cube state requires more than 20 moves, so we know that God's Number is 20.

Knowing that a speedcuber will only need to use at most 20 moves to solve a given cube does not let them know how to go about solving it. God's Algorithm is the way to solve the cube that always takes the shortest route, using the least number of moves. While Richard Karf's algorithm for solving the cube has been shown to be optimal, it is not clear that it is God's Algorithm for the cube in a way meaningful to a speedcuber.

Interactivity

SLUG Nº. 2: PONG

At each level of detail or "turtle" we can similarly describe more complex interactive content, with some special precisions that enable us to deal with the complexities of an interactive system – particularly its dependence on user, player, or audience input. To elaborate each of these levels, we'll take as example the classic video game (and in fact the classic "example of a video game"): *Pong*. Let's walk through the various levels of notational detail available to us, and look at the ways that an interactive notation might have some special qualities to attend to and benefit from.

First Turtle: Sometimes a Sentence or Two is Enough

At the most basic level of notational abstraction, we have a very brief high-level description, invoking familiar concepts and using little jargon, which could be either written or verbal; something like the "Fluxus notation" of sentence-as-score. Quite similarly, a game design can be as simple as a sentence of instructions - the game's rules. Recently and notably, gameplay experimenters Hide&Seek created a series of what they call "Tiny Games", introducing the concept with the tagline "Sometimes a sentence or two is enough."[1] Tiny Games are gameplay compositions consisting of a few simple rules designed (or at least adapted) for a very specific location and context. For example, one Tiny Game called *Eye Contact* is meant to be played in a crowd on a terrace in a public place:
"A game for two or more players. Race from one end of the terrace to the other. You're only allowed to move while you're making eye contact with someone else."
For more complex, interactive, and digital pieces like our *Pong* example, the short verbal description is not enough to encapsulate all the rules, and instead might be considered an "elevator pitch" for the game. Unlike a Fluxus score, which itself is considered sufficient information to perform the piece it represents, a short text notation of a video game is not sufficient to bring the game of *Pong* into existence. It is simply sufficient to give an adult with sufficient command of language and knowledge of culture a basic idea of the game and its functions. So what makes it a notation at all? And what's special about an interactive high-level notation? For an interactive piece, at this extremely high level it is crucial to speak specifically of what the interactant (usually, but not always, a human) must actively do in order to interact with the work.

Interactivity

Hide&Seek, Eye Contact, 2012. Photo: Paul Bennun

As actions, these descriptions center around descriptive verbs. In the case of *Pong*, consider the following:

> "*Pong* is a simple two-player competitive game resembling Table Tennis (Ping-Pong), with each player occupying either the left or right side of a rectangular screen. You play by moving a short bar called a "paddle" up and down along the far edge of your side, in order to hit a bouncing ball and keep it from passing off your side of the screen. Whenever you block the ball, you also send it bouncing back across the screen, and try to cause the other player to miss it."

The short verbal notation of an interactive work should include the *Who*, the *What* and the *Where* of the work; *who* is interacting, *what* the interactants do and *where* the action takes place. By comparison, here is a text about *Pong* which is technically correct, but is far less useful as a notation:

> "*Pong* is an arrangement of pixels moving on a screen. A ball represented by four pixels aligned in a square moves around the screen and sometime makes numbers increment."

Next Turtle: Visual Overview

At a certain level quite early on in a detailed notation or description of an interactive work, it becomes necessary to use representational visuals. In screen-based (or at least screen-including) works such as a video game, that representation will often be an analog of the screen itself. In a spacialized work (for instance, David Rokeby's *Very Nervous System*), the visual notation will more likely take the form of an architectural rendering - a diagram with reference to the physical world. And of course, many works will have (and have notated) elements of both.

Let's look at our *Pong* example again. In the notation below, a rectangle represents the screen of a television or computer, which is the player's visual interface - the only means through which interactants get feedback to the game state. Lines, arrows, dots, and text in the notation represent both the on-screen information, and the meta information about what is seen. Color and line style are used (in the original) to distinguish the markings which are representative of the screen itself, and those which are notations referring to the behavior of the system. For instance, black markings in this *Pong* diagram indicate the on-screen elements themselves: the solid black rectangle represents the boundaries of the playing field, the dotted center line is the symbolic boundary of each player's side of the court, the small black bars are the two player "paddles," the black square is the ball, and the numbers are the score. Other information about the behavior of the system is described using a system of colors. The "walls" are shown and notated in green, the "goals" in pink, and the motion of the player paddles in brown. Of course these color choices are somewhat arbitrary - the important point is that some sort of meta-information (color, font, line style, etc) is used to distinguish different types of information and help visually organize (separate or connect) elements of the notation.

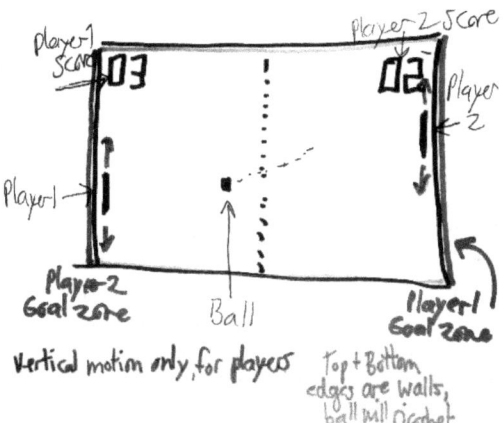

Pong as an annotated screen shot.

This notation type is very good at explaining elements of the system

Interactivity

which are continually present in the experience. In a work which often changes its means of feedback or has different interaction "states," a notation will need multiple renderings in order to describe each of them. If the interaction feedback is in constant flux with little or no consistency from moment to moment, then the screen diagram may not be a very useful form of notation for that work.

Next Turtle: Storyboard

Another type of visual notation is the storyboard or keyframe animation. The interactive work is represented in multiple consecutive "frames" representing the same experience captured at different moments in time. Notations of this kind are more useful in a non-interactive linear work, to describe in a few snapshots the course of action over a longer time. In interactive work, a storyboard such as this one from our *Pong* example below, might be most useful for explaining what did or could happen during the course of one playthrough of the game.& As in the annotated screenshot style, a visual (colorful) distinction is made between the elements of the screen itself (here shown in thick black line) and the meta-information, which here represents the behaviors of elements such as the motion of the ball, and the change of the score number.

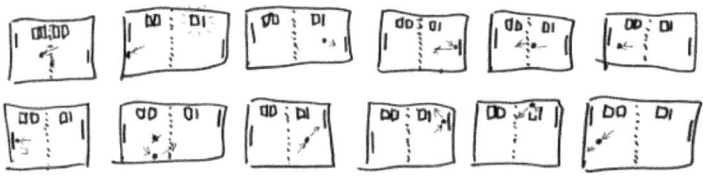

Pong as a series of key frames with dynamics.

In storyboard/keyframes of this type, it's important to think about the proper granularity of the sequence. What moments in the experience are important to capture in the portrayal of change over time? Are there extremes of motion which would be meaningful for explaining the entire gesture, such as with animation keyframes? Or is it necessary to break down motions into smaller increments to show the process of changes taking place, and allowing the human mind to re-create the motions without much interpolation?
All in all, the storyboard description of *Pong* shown here is at a rather fine level of detail. This level might be useful, for instance, to notate the desired or expected physics behavior of the ball bouncing around the

court in order to communicate with game engine designers, or it might be a useful visual way to describe the typical progress of a game to someone who has not played it, such as the visual design team.

Next Turtle: Control/Interface Diagram

The aim of this level of notation is showing the details of how the interactant will express themselves. What is their range of possible action? This will vary based on platform, even within the same work.

Missing in the screen-based visual representation of a work is one very crucial element: the means of interacting with it -the language of human gestures or actions that makes the work actually interactive. A notation of an interactive system without some discussion of the interface would be grossly incomplete. Of course just about any type of human motion could be recognized by an interactive system and turned into a reaction within the system, whether that action is "freestanding" or in relation to a physical object. Conscious interaction ranges from the tiniest muscle movement, such as a subtle touch on a sensitive touchpad or the twitch of an iris or eyelid, as in the *EyeWriter* and other more conventional assistance technologies, to full-body swinging and jumping as in many sensor-based artwork, or pushing and pulling the massive levers inside the control booth of a construction crane.

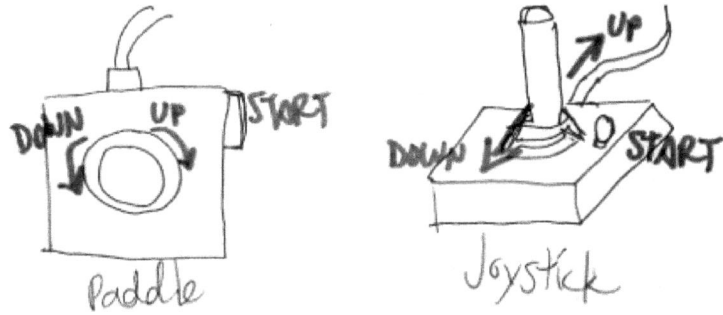

Interaction possibilities for two classic Pong controllers.

In the case of *Pong*, these diagrams notate two of the earliest and best-recognized physical interfaces to the game: the paddle and the joystick. The "paddle" controller is in fact so closely associated with the game *Pong* because it was created and sold as a controller specifically for the earliest versions of the television game. This explains the unusual naming of the controller, which bears no visual similarity to the

Interactivity

traditional analog table tennis paddle after which it is named.

In these two particular *Pong* control illustrations, the controller itself is depicted in a clean-lined representation, while the specific actions available to the player are annotated in bold. We can see from the two side-by-side representations that the user's actions are very simple, and that the two controllers, though using different directions of movement (rotating around a central axis, or bi-directional in a line) are accomplishing the same actions within the game interface (moving the player's paddle up and down along the edge of the court.) This abstraction between specific physical interfaces, and system behaviors, is one of the most important reasons to specifically include an interface diagram in the notation of any interactive system.

Next Turtle: Flow Charts and State Charts

Flow charts and state diagrams are perhaps the notation methods most closely associated with the design of interactive work, in that they are the simplest and most comprehensible notation systems which attempt to capture the system's logic: the cause and effect of specific interactions themselves. They show how the choices that the interactant make over the course of the interaction session will change the work, and how it will respond to the interactant with new information that allows them to make further choices.

Within these categories of interaction charts there are multiple standards used in various professions to improve legibility and continuity of meaning. These standards usually include specific shapes such as rectangles, diamonds, and ovals to communicate certain types of meaning such as decisions and outcomes. Depending on the need of communicating through the diagram with different groups of people (and on their familiarity with the standard), it may make sense to use these standardized notation systems, though it's not necessary.

This flow chart for *Pong* is an example of an attempt to describe its "game loop." Each round or match of the game is described from the standpoint of the ball's behavior, and the game's reaction to its state.

The end of the flowchart is reached, the current match is done, and if the current match led to the winning point scored, then the entire game session is complete. Notably, lower levels of the gameplay, such as the physics controlling the speed and direction of the ball, are not dealt with at this level of detail. It's noted at certain moments that the ball will change direction and velocity, but the calculations behind these changes are not explained in any detail that would allow accurate prediction. Note that this allows us to have different implementations that might include factors such as a slice play adding extra sideways

13. Slug nº. 2: Pong

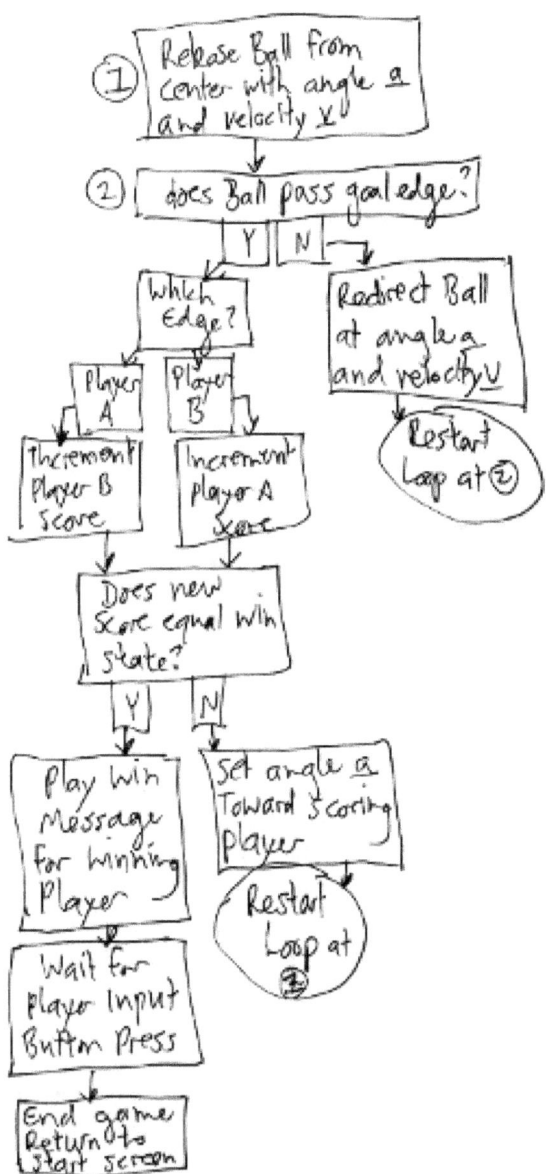

Pong as a flowchart giving a description of behaviour.

Interactivity

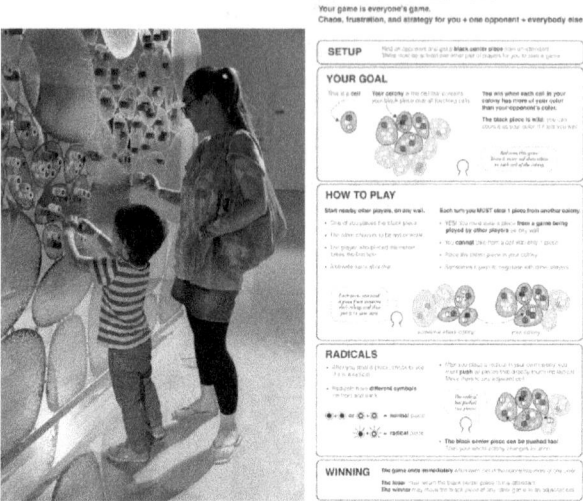

Nathalie Pozzi and Eric Zimmerman, "Rules for Interference," 2012.

velocity to the ball, or having the simplest version where the sideways velocity is constant, only changing in direction.

Next Turtle: Rules

In an analog interactive piece which depends more on player/interactant behavior for the system to run (for instance, *Pictionary*, or *Tennis*, or our *Tiny Games* example above), the collection of step-by-step rules and various "if-then" cases could be considered synonymous with the algorithm of the interactive work itself. Rule descriptions can be text only, or a combination of text and images. In general they are written as commands to the interactant, instructing them what to do from moment to moment and in particular cases (which are states of the system).

For instance in the large-scale analog game *Interference* by Nathalie Pozzi and Eric Zimmerman, the rules were described to players with text and images on a sheet of paper that was available near the game's playing area. The notation consists of close-up images of the playing field and pieces, along with expected steps of action, and even small pictograms showing moments in an example play session.

In digital interactive content, it can also be useful to notate the work using the sequence of rules, and this method is particularly used to teach the behavior of the system to a new interactant. A special variation on listing the rules is a tutorial, in which each step of the rules is accompanied by an interactive opportunity for the interactant to try the specific rule. Since digital interactive work can sense the interactant's input, it can determine whether the interactant has successfully understood the rule and move on to the next.

In our *Pong* example, a notation of the rules (written or spoken outside the game) would simply say "Control the paddle by pushing your joystick up and down," while a tutorial inside the game might, after delivering the same information, wait to receive input from the game that the player had successfully moved their paddle all the way to the top and the bottom of the navigable area before continuing to the next step in the instructions. In this way, interaction itself becomes part of the notation.

Next Turtle: Game Code

The software code underlying any digital work is of course a type of notation. However for the purposes of our discussion, we feel that the interesting examination is of the less precise, more interpretable and generally readable (not requiring specialist knowledge of particular syntax) levels of notation. For that reason, we have set aside discussions of Pseudocode, scripting languages, high level computer languages, machine languages, and the like. However all of these types of detailed notation could be fruitful areas of inquiry in future work.

Next Turtle: Notating the Play of a Game

Finally it's worth looking at codified ways of describing the moment-to-moment play within a single instance of a single interactive work. Like other media (music, dance), notation can serve to record the actual process of the work in action. Moment-to-moment notations are very useful for games that are heavy in strategy and do not place significant value on the quality of physical movement. In certain strategic games this type of notation actually can become quite simple, as all of the actions are easily converted into discrete symbols. Knowledge of the game's rules, combined with a list of the actions, can render a precise impression of the session. This is especially notable with classic games like Chess and Bridge, and very likely contributes to their communicability and popularity through time. Other games with complex physical structures are sometimes notated through a series of images or diagrams of movement. For instance the game Go can be portrayed as a sequence showing each move by the two alternating

Interactivity

players. The sport of American Football is often notated (especially for training purposes) with a book of strategic illustrations called a Playbook.

By comparison, as a thought experiment, we could imagine that it is possible to real-time-notate an interactive work such as *Pong*, which uses simple physical controls in real time. For instance, what if a joystick controller being used in a game of *Pong* were also connected to an old-fashioned mechanical plotter (such as those used in seismographs), with the paper roll moving at a constant speed? Through this method, you could track a player's vertical path over the course of an entire game, with fast and sudden moves creating sharp inclines, and slow moves creating gradual slopes. Indeed, it would be interesting to use the output as a musical score!

1. http://hideandseek.net/projects/tiny-games/

A Few Specimens

INTRODUCTION TO THE EXAMPLES

In contemporary artistic practise most of the time artists invent a score for just one specific purpose. This goes so far that, even in music, few pieces are played more than once. As mentioned in the *Steal this Notation* chapter, artists feel rightly free to grab whatever they need from any existing notation systems to express themselves. In many ways during these process new symbols appear and are fed back into existing systems, thereby changing and expanding them.

A good image for that process is the cathedral and the bazaar (as *stolen* from the famous essay by free software advocate Eric S. Raymond). Let us say the cathedral is the classical music notation developed over thousands of years and the bazaar are all the individual approaches to creating a score. The bazaar is a teeming mass of independent actors, all following their own ideas and desires, taking on projects and abandoning them when finished or losing interest, recycling the parts left lying around in ways unintended by the original constructors and attaching whatever they like to whatever they can as they see fit. The cathedral is the system that "just works," where one is allowed to enter and do what one must, but there is no way to attach a rope to the wall or assemble a small stall in an unused corner. The cathedral does what it should and new functionality is a rare thing.

But the cathedral and the bazaar are continuously influencing each other. The cathedral absorbs parts of the bazaar and curiosities inside the cathedral start to get new meanings in the bazaar. There are no radical changes in either arena, attempts at denoting innovation are more like setting markers in a time continuum. The cathedral reacts slowly and ponderously with due regard for tradition and backwards compatibility. The bazaar is a teeming mass of tiny increments where every development can be seen to derive from a number of other developments, remixing them in interesting ways through unconcious empathy, explicit adaption and outright theft. At some point the quantitative difference is large enough to feel like a qualitative one, and someone gets the credit for innovation, regardless of the fact that 99% of the elements existed previously.

The following examples show artistic approaches towards notating their work for different purposes. Many of these examples borrow notational techniques from their own and other fields or misuse techniques that they find interesting. These ad-hoc techniques are very carefully rooted in the bazaar, and some might also say bizarre, with explanations needed. This is an important aspect of any non-cathedral, and perhaps many cathedral, notations. The semantics of the symbols are unclear and require explanation or negotiation. The negotiation may be one sided as when the artist makes statements about what exactly each symbol and connection means, which will be the case with more developed works (e.g. *sitting in my chair*). Other negotiations might be more explorative, being developed by colleagues working together to discuss a problem and wanting to be talking about certain aspects as they arise in the discussion (e.g. *Formocracy* or *The Black Box Sessions*). A further category might be taken from some of the less well defined musical scores, where the score might appear to be little more than a postcard of a painting or mess of lines and colour swatches, where the performers have to negotiate how they will go about interpreting the score without being able to interact with the creator of the score (e.g. *Isorhythmic Variations*).

The following examples will unpack some of these issues and hopefully illuminate them in interesting ways. Many of the examples introduced previously could be moved here - this collection of examples is the melting pot from which insights and inspirations may arise.

HACKING CHOREOGRAPHY SERIES (2012)

Kate Sicchio[1] is a choreographer, media artist, researcher and performer whose work includes dance performances, installations, web and video projects. In her research she looks into parallels between code and choreography as well as to find implications in areas such as live notation and live coding. This chapter is based upon her presentation at the 2012 Data Ecologies symposium in Linz.
Most of her work involves live realtime projection in live performance, which she programs, choreographs and performs. She normally creates all the elements of the pieces. In her head she doesn't separate these things - they're all choreography to her, including sitting and coding. Her project developed out of the idea of how does code become choreography. Laban's notation system focused on "the body" not the general space of the performance. Sicchio thinks in terms of relationships as choreography and is interested in finding new ways to hack choreographic pieces.

Notation in Live Compositional Processes

Hacking choreography beta v.02 was an experiment at University of Lincoln. There Sicchio developed a series of experiments to test out some theories.

> *"A choreographic object is not a substitute for the body, but rather an alternative site for the understanding of potential instigation and organization of action to reside. Ideally, choreographic ideas in this form would draw an attentive, diverse readership that would eventually understand and, hopefully, champion the innumerable manifestations, old and new, of choreographic thinking" (William Forsythe 2009).*

So, while not substituting for the body, there is still a relationship between the body and choreography, it's just not centred around the body anymore like Laban's work and the focus has moved a little away from it. Forsythe proposes that choreography is a way of thinking. One thing which Sicchio doesn't quite agree with is his use of the word 'organisation'. She likes to think of choreography as relationships rather than organisation.
Within her own work she wanted to find something similar which she could do with scores, and start to change them in realtime. With her video tracking systems she jacked a Kinect and was interested in how she could hack the movement system. She began with existing scores,

A Few Specimens

taking this as the code and then changed it to make the performance. Below is the first hack she started with, taken from the Fluxus Performance Workbook.

Performance Piece # 8 by Alison Knowles (1965)

Divide a variety of objects into two groups. Each group is labeled "everything." These groups may include several people. There is a third division of the stage, empty of objects, labeled "nothing." Each of the objects is "something." One performer combines and activates the objects as follows for any desired duration of time:

1 Something with everything
2 Something with nothing
3 Something with something
4 Everything with everything
5 Everything with nothing
6 Nothing with nothing

A Fluxus textual piece.

In Sicchio's performance[2] she labeled objects and created her structures with paper and stickers. The first part was her following the score, interpreting it rather than hacking it and she used audience members within the piece as the score said you could. She did this with very little preparation, the idea being that the composition would emerge in realtime. This is because she wanted the hack to be in realtime. There isn't a lot of choice within the score of what to do, so she wanted to make her decisions in a realtime, pressured situation. The initial way she decided to hack it was to rip up the paper and categories, and making new ones out of the language which existed. She ended the piece when she got frustrated with not knowing what she had done, fed up with making the decisions in realtime.

Hacking Choreography

The next choreographic hack was when she made her own code. It's made to look like JavaScript, but also made so a dancer could read it.

```
/Dance/
set up ()                                              Run ()
{                                                      {
dancer a centre, right                                 Move1
dancer b centre, left                                  Move4
}                                                      Move4
movement ()                                            Move1
{                                                      Move2
move1 (dancer a = rotate) (dancer b = jump)            Move3
move2 (dancer a = brush) (dancer b = lie down)         Move1
move3 (dancer a = push) (dancer b = run)               Move2
move4 (dancer a = step ) (dancer b = kneel)            Move3
}                                                      Move4
choreography ()                                        }
{
if (dancer a = rotate right 180)
jump = 2 feet to 1
if (dancer b = travels)
brush = right foot
{
```

Choreographical scoring in pseudocode.

15. Hacking Choreography series (2012)

With a collection of instructions that explain each move, and a series of moves defined in a linear fashion, a whole dance piece can be constructed in pseudocode. One the dancers have learnt the various moves and the instructions for various reactions, the coded series of moves might be easier to memorise and perform appropriately.

```
/hack/
{
if (dancer b = kneel)
dancer a = kneel
if (dancer a = rotate)
dancer b = rotate opposite
direction
}
```

Pseudocode looking at reactive choreography - introducing the hack.

Finally she had a setup with two dancers, defining the movement she was interested in. The dancers interpreted this. The choreography section (incomplete in this listing) is the collection of relationships created for the piece. She then gave the dancers an order to run the process, the Run() routine. She gave the code to them the day before the performance without any other instructions so they had to work the details out themselves. Halfway through the performance Kate put up new instructions, this was the *hack*, and the dancers had to change their relationships depending on this. Kate did actually give them the hack an hour before the performance, she they knew it was coming but they had to figure it out in the moment.

For the performance[3] the dancers performed it with the movements straight through, then with the relationships and then they performed the hack as it appeared on the screen.

One of Kate's colleagues in the computer science department got very excited about the piece and wrote the code up in JavaScript as opposed to Kate's pseudoscript, but it is very similar.

Whether the resulting code can be executed in any performance-meaningful way is an open question, but the code will produce a written document that describes the dance piece as a series of moves. A question arises: which notation of the dance, the code or the resulting sequence of moves, is the more useful notation? Which will give a more interesting performance? To what degree is the breakage of the performance by the introduction of the hack and the resulting glitching the actual performance? Would a perfect performance of this piece be wrong by definition?

The last piece in the series[4] that Sicchio made was about the dancer being a hacker, where she gave verbal instructions. What was

A Few Specimens

```
script type="text/javascript"
function hack()
{
if (dancer_b=='kneel')
dancer_a='kneel'
if (dancer_a=='rotate')
dancer_b='rotate opposite direction to a'
}

function update()
{
hack();
document.write("
"+dancer_a+" "+dancer_b+"
");
}

function setup() { dancer_a='center, right'; dancer_b='center, left'; update(); }
function move1() { dancer_a='rotate'; dancer_b='jump'; update(); }
function move2() { dancer_a='brush'; dancer_b='lie down'; update(); }
function move3() { dancer_a='push'; dancer_b='run'; update(); }
function move4() { dancer_a='step'; dancer_b='kneel'; update(); }

function run()
{
setup();
move1();
move4();
move1();
move2();
move3();
move1();
move2();
move3();
move4();
}

run()
/script
```

Javascript
Duncan Rowland

Executable JavaScript version of the choreographical pseudocode.

interesting about this one was, that the score started with what Sicchio was saying, but then the dancer had to slowly change what she was doing so she wasn't doing what Sicchio was instructing. The score isn't what Sicchio was saying at all, just at the beginning, making the dancer the hacker. This experience led her to a community of live coders. What she has in common with them is live compositional processes, in that there is some kind of system or score that is set up and within it there is a frame from change. There is also a transparency about it, with the projection of code.

This led her to work with Alex McLean on a piece called *Prism II*.

Real Time Notation

In *Prism II* they tried to build up a feedback loop between the two performers. Sicchio would do set movements which she had pre-coded and were projected behind her and McLean was using his system which was projected too. Unfortunately (or perhaps not!) he had brought the wrong one for the performance - an unintended glitch that forced more active live coding.

She would change dynamics and qualities of the movements whilst performing and he would change the dynamics and qualities of the sound he was producing, which would then in turn make her change what she was doing; this created a feedback loop. Both the code sets were projected side by side. This was completely un-rehearsed and most of Sicchio's choreography doesn't use sound so this was a significant challenge. They plan to perform it again in a rehearsed manner. There is

15. Hacking Choreography series (2012)

Real Time Notation interactions; Prism II performance shots.

a score but this live compositional process is the priority.
Kate Sicchio is taking part in other choreographic hacks. One at the Arnolfini in Bristol, with a live notation[5] group who look at where live code and live art meet. She is one of the live coders, and the artists are going to draw a score, which she follows live as it is created.

1. Website http://sicchio.com/
2. *Hacking Choreography v.01*, http://vimeo.com/36369236
3. *Hacking Choreography beta v.02*, http://vimeo.com/36369338
4. *Hacking Choreography beta v.03*, http://vimeo.com/36369416
5. LNU performance research group. http://livenotation.org/

A Few Specimens

BLACK BOX SESSIONS (2008)

Alex Davies[1] is a sound & video artist. His work spans a diverse range of media including film, network, realtime audio-visual manipulations and responsive installations.

Time´s Up[2] is an art connective [sic!] based in Linz, Austria. Founded in 1996, Time's Up has its principal locus in the Linz harbour of Austria. The mission of the connective mission is to investigate the ways in which people interact with and explore their physical surroundings as a complete context, discovering, learning and communicating as they do. Alex Davies and Time's Up have collaborated extensively since 1999.

Working Out the Possibilities

The installation was presented to visitors as follows:

> *A mediated installation environment which offers the public a distinct perspective on live performances.*
> *Time's Up and Alex Davies have curated a series of performances presented by 11 national and international performers who will be present throughout the course of the exhibition. The performances take place in a pitch black room and are viewed by individual audience members via an infra-red camera and monitor system. This unique environment shifts the relationship between performer and spectator and challenges dominant visual perception.*

Only one audience member at a time (usually!) goes into a completely black environment where the only light source is a hole 15mm in diameter. Looking through the hole a screen can be seen showing an infrared image of them in the space. The audience sees themselves from behind as well as other things around them, including the performers apparently walking in and performing in the dark next to them. The audience member can experience the performance only through the camera-screen channel.

The interesting thing was that Time's Up and Alex Davies had created a 'green box' scenario where they made recordings of the performers acting as if they were in the dark. These green box recordings were then treated so that they had no background (green removal) and made to look like they had been filmed with the same camera as the infrared surveillance camera that was watching the audience members from behind. Then the audience member could see themselves in the pitch black space and could only see the pre-recorded performers through the technology of the camera and the screen.

A Few Specimens

Four examples of visitors interacting with performers as seen through the infrared peephole.

If the audience member left the screen, they were alone in a pitch dark room which, after having the bright screen in one eye, was subjectively even darker than before. Attempts to find the performer were destined to fail, as they were not there, but the confusion of darkness and the multichannel sound system helped create a convincing illusion.

The performance recordings were planned to start after the audience member had arrived at the peephole. Two sensors in the entrance tunnel registered the movement and direction of a visitor, a third sensor registered whether they were standing in front of the peephole. It was assumed that the audience member was alone, this was stated at the entrance and a red-green light combination was used to indicate whether a new audience member could enter.

The crew wanted to be able to synchronize it all so it worked properly, leading them to sit down and work out everything which could happen in the space, including playing the video and merging it with the live footage from the camera. To help realise this, they created a diagram showing the ideal things which would happen and the not so ideal:

Some explanation of the terminology used on the flowchart might help understanding. The bottom right shows the Black Box from above. A visitor (V in the rest of the diagram) passes the LL_1 sensor then the LL_2 sensor as they come into the Black Box and then stand in front of the screen. On the left side of the diagram there is the comment "nothing" indicating that nothing is going on. In this state, the green lamp is on. The correct next action is for a visitor to enter, triggering the LL_1 sensor and moving to state "V in LL" where the lamp turns to red. If they turn around and leave, not liking the dark, the state changes back to "nothing" and the lamp goes green. The lamp remains red in every state other than "nothing" as only in the "nothing" state does the

16. Black Box Sessions (2008)

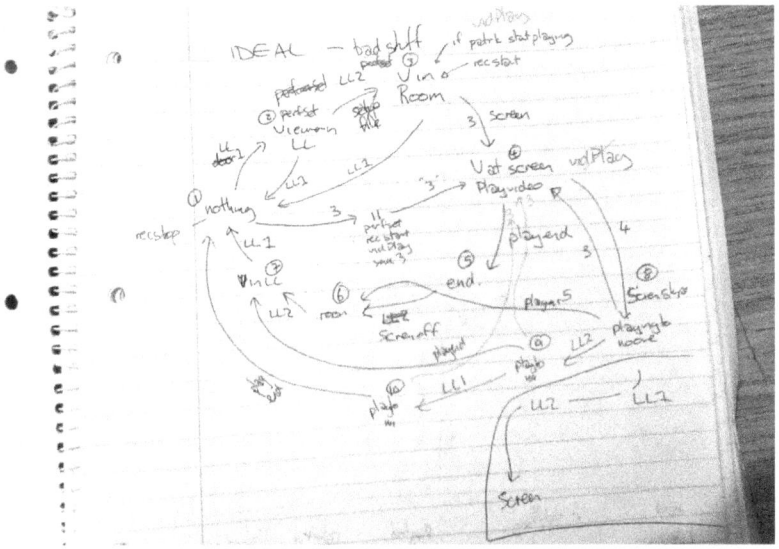

A flowchart for the Black Box Sessions describing possible eventualities from all possible "states" of the system - where the system thinks the visitor is based upon various sensor inputs and system events.

system believe there is nobody in the Black Box.

Normally the visitor then triggers the LL2 sensor, so the state is "V in room" before the screen sensor is triggered indicating that the visitor is looking into the screen hole. Then the state becomes "V at screen" and the video is played. When the video finishes, "playend" triggers, the visitor leaves the screen and then triggers the LL2 and then LL1 as they leave and the system state returns to "nothing" so the lamp is green and the next audience member can enter.

The rest of the diagram is filled with lines and states indicating the ways that the visitor and the system are doing things that have not been planned for. Perhaps the visitor leaves the screen before the video finishes and wanders around in the dark. Or even leaves the Black Box completely. Perhaps some sensor triggers unexpectedly. The discussion amongst the crew tried to work out what to do in all these cases.

This diagram was developed in order to enabl the Max MSP patch to do everything at the correct time. They also created a numbered diagram to assist with working out this process, as the diagram above is filled with all sorts of human readable information.

A Few Specimens

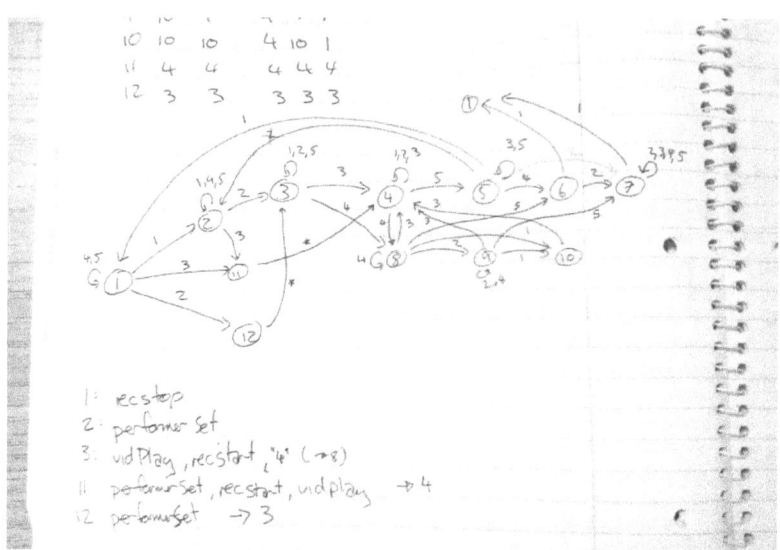

An abstracted form of the above state diagram made ready for entering into the program.

Black Box Sessions is a relatively simple piece, with few enough states that it was able to be analysed on an A4 page. The process of discussing the piece and its dynamics on a page with human readable comments and annotated arcs between named states made analysing the system feasible and helped work out what the appropriate dynamics should be when the unexpected occured. Translating this to the machine readable situation of a series of rows of numbers, one row per state, made the dynamics readable and implementable by the Max/MSP patch. This series of translations, from the human readable state diagram to the numbered version to the array of numbers to the code that would implement the state machine dynamics, is error prone but given that the implementation is correct, the three notations are structurally isomorphic.

1. Bio and other details at http://schizophonia.com/
2. Website: http://timesup.org

SITTING IN MY CHAIR (2001)

Elisabeth Schimana[1] has been working as a composer, performer and radio artist since 1983. She has ongoing cooperations with the Austrian Kunstradio and the Theremin Center Moscow. She also focusses on research in the field of women, art and technology. 2005 she founded IMA (Institute for Media Archeology)[2]

Notation for an Interactive Performance

The armchair addressed in the title is a very special chair, not a synonym for chairs in general, but exactly this chair whose characteristic screech was the beginning point for the musical design of sitting in my chair. The acoustic material consists of these screeches, which were recorded as audio data and then (re)played during the performance. In this very chair the sounds are manipulated simply through the movement of the hands. It's not a coincidence that Elisabeth Schimana developed this piece in Moscow at the electronic Institute of the Tschaikovski Conservatory, an Institute with the proud name Theremin Center. As Schimana discovered the Theremin years ago, it wasn't so much the sounds that interested her, but the body and stage presence of this antique instrument that is played without touching. What is the body doing on stage in the age of electronic music? This question with its area of tension between Kraftwerk's Puppets and today's expressively maltreated laptops is uncoiled again and again by Elisabeth Schimana in her work. The Theremin surfaced as the perfect challenge: for whatever reason the thereminic antenna technology with its transparent magnetic field as interface is used - as direct sound control or as trigger for completely different mechanisms - it provides the electronic musician a necessity for a physical presence. The physical motion on stage as a category is again scrutinised if in sitting in my chair the artist sits almost motionless in her chair. With minimal finger, hand, and head movements, the dense snarl of chair screeches are erased while the stringent lighting is changed one field after the other with every erasing procedure.
(nina ross)

The Score

Performance time: Is dependent on the performer's actions. Mininum time would be 160 seconds.
Chair sound matrix: Is the heart of the piece. The target is to erase via the theremin sensor interface each of the 48 cells. Each cell is connected to the light matrix and any state of the matrix is generating information for the panning and amplitude progress.

A Few Specimens

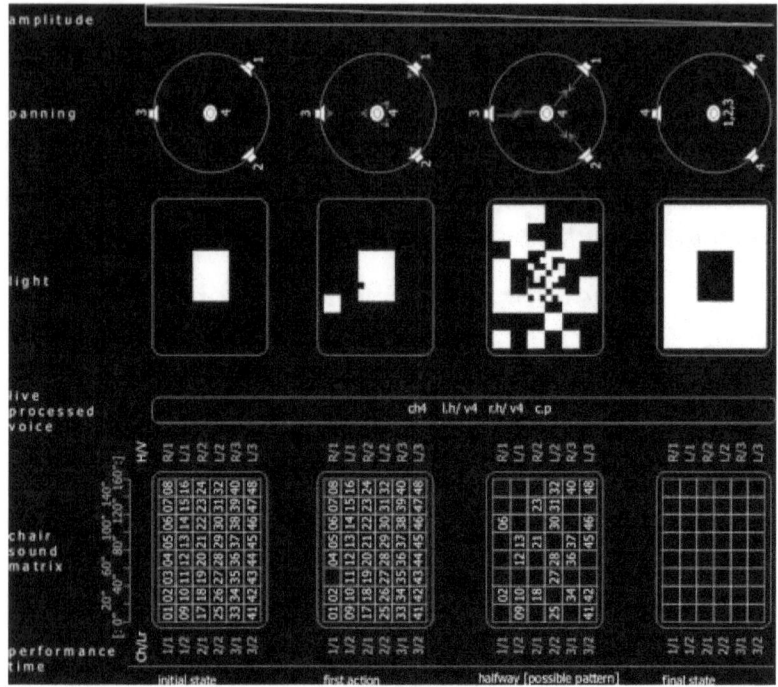

ch=output channel, lr=soundlayer, r.h=right hand, l.h=left hand, c.p=center position, v=velocity of the hands' movements

The Score of the piece, showing the central elements of the composition as key frames.

Live processed voice: The voice is free, not connected to the matrix and processed by granular synthesis, which generates three slightly different soundstreams out of one vocal input.

Light: has to be considered as two overlapping layers of sqares each of them divided in the raster of 8x6. The 48 patterns are generated depending on the information generated by the chair sound matrix. The focus is on the changing light rays inside the light cone, rather than on the projection on the floor. The only possibility to make this cone visible is to produce a lot of smoke. In the final state the performer is disappearing in light.

Panning and amplitude: Both parameters depend on the relative time information (how many cells are erased) generated by the chair sound matrix. You can consider the circle as the space for the audience, chair sounds are moving to the center mixed into one stream while the granular stream is moving outside and splitting up into three streams. At the same time the amplitude is decreasing to zero.

Chair sound layers: All layers contain recorded chair sounds from the performance chair without any additional sound processing. Layer 1 contains continous chair sounds and layer 2 peak fragments of layer 1. All three output channels differ from one other. The looped soundstreams' duration is free in time not depending on the matrix time, which results connected to the matrix time in a permanent shifting of the material.

Sensor Stuff and Engines

Velocity of the hands' movements: After experimenting it turned out that it makes sense to divide the hand movements into 4 different velocities, from v1 slow movement to v4 fast movement, to control the system. Velocities 1 to 3 are related to the soundlayers, with each action one cell will be erased - 20 seconds of sound disappear - the light pattern is changing.

Velocity of the hand movements and center position: R.h/v4 is switching voice on and off, l.h/v4 is switching between the granular synthesis, parameters grain duration and grain density. These two parameters are controlled by the movements of the center position, very tiny movements with the head and the upper part of the body.

The body has to be tuned: In the antennas' sphere of action the zero point has to be found to tune the body to the system. All data generated by the performer's body movements are derived by two identical thereminsensors located to the performer's left and right.

Sensor antennas: The construction of both sensors is based on the theremin principle: to change the frequency of the ultrasonic oscillator by the capacitance of the performers body, hand or whatever goes close to the antenna. The audio frequency sound is produced then by heterodyning the outputs of two ultrasonic oscillators. The fixed oscillator operates in the region of 350 KHz with the above mentioned variable oscillator being above this frequency, the difference equaling the frequency of the sound being produced. Allthough that would only make a minute difference, the theremin sensor cleverly has two very high frequency oscillators. That way, even a 0.05% change in the variable oscillator can be substantial at audio frequency. Enough, with good design, to give a range of several octaves.

Analysing the sensor signals: Two audio range signals from the sensors are producing the stereo input for the computer. A specially developed MAX/MSP patch analyses the input signal's pitches, converts them into floating point values and produces filtering and scaling to achieve a

Initial state, photo from the performance at Musikprotokoll / Graz 2001.

stable and linear mapping of the measured data over the whole range of possible distances. In *sitting in my chair* the patch is interpreting the derived floating point data as velocity (increasing and decreasing values over time) of the hands' movements.

Center position: It means, that if the performer is sitting in the point of the equal distance from both sensors, they produce equal signals and taking the difference between the values of the analysed signals and scaling them we can get values, reflecting even the slightest deviations of the body from the central position.

Generating midi data: Several threshhold- presets are set in the MAX/MSP patch to produce the proper MIDI data to connect with other programs and machines.

The kyma engine: Is responsible for the chair sound matrix, live voice processing and sound streams mixing. Based on the received MIDI information and the circular time pointer position (0 seconds to 160 seconds) the targeted chair sound matrix cell index is calculated. This cell index is deactivated which results in immediate sound cancellation. At the same time the cell index is passed down the pipeline to the NATO component.

NATO: Is an extention of the MAX/MSP program. It produces the appropriate video images to be projected creating the light cone.

In-between states. Photo from the performance at Musikprotokoll / Graz 2001.

Credits

sitting in my chair was produced by Musikprotokoll in cooperation with the Theremin Center Moscow.
Elisabeth Schimana: composition, sound design, vocals, live performer, Andre Smirnov: instrument design and nato programming, Yuri Spitsin: sound design and kyma programming.

1. http://elise.at
2. http://ima.or.at/

A Few Specimens

FORMOCRACY (2012)

Lev Ledit and Andreas Dekrout both work at Game Gestalt[1], a game design company based in Vienna. Lev Ledit teaches game design at several institutions and universities, he also is the CEO of Game Gestalt. Andreas Dekrout has a background in legal academic work, social entrepreneurship and activism. He is the project manager of *formocracy*.

When the Map became the Landscape

The project *formocracy* is about the creation of real-world political pressure for desired change by members of the online community with integrated mechanics producing precise action-oriented orders which are backed by the legitimacy of democratic processes. All this is powered by the psychological mechanics taken from game design, to motivate users to "play" for a higher purpose while simply satisfying their urge for joy.

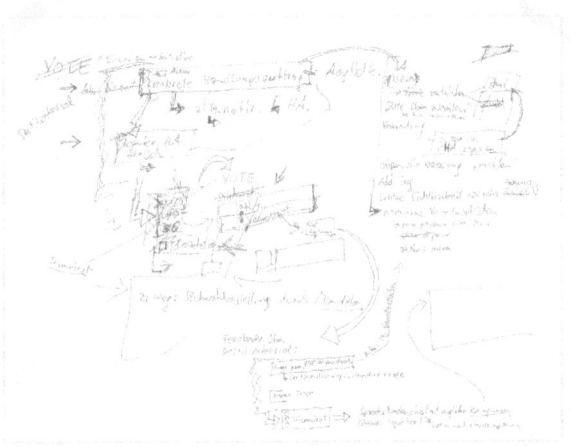

Figure 1. A first draft of a flowchart. Multiple languages, arrows, boxes and anything else we could find giving an impromptu notational system.

This example follows the path of development from the initial "let's do that thing", existing only as an exciting goal in our minds. Via a trial and error phase of trying to develop a working structure capable of achieving that goal we came to a notation system. The evolution of that

A Few Specimens

notation system and the feedback effects upon the form of notation systems used at several stages had an enabling effect on the further development of the project as a whole. As the structure became clearer and clearer in our thoughts so did also the way we would draw sketches and charts.

The image in Figure 1 shows one of the first drafts for the decision-making part of Formocracy. During the first few (full) days of discussion and turning the idea which was later to become *formocracy* around in our heads the mechanics and logical sequences were drafted out on a piece of paper (in a restaurant during dinner). Without prior agreement on any specific notation system, we used what felt natural to us. Language (German), lines, arrows, wave-lines, boxes, and so forth. Using this intuitive notation we were able to work on what turned out to be less clear than expected and could edit and change the concept at the same time.

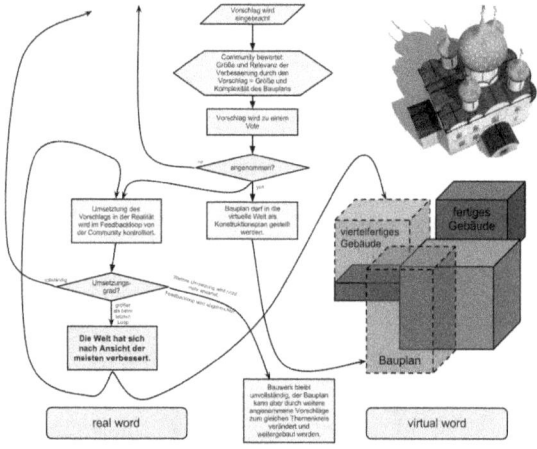

Figure 2. A formalised draft of the high level game process as a flowchart. The diagram has gained formal structure, however a lot of explanation is embedded in the document within which it is contained.

Figure 2 shows a flowchart for the logic sequence for a proposal within the *formocracy* system in the virtual and real world. After the most essential questions and challenges were solved the need to communicate the planned flow of action arose. The formalised flowchart in Figure 2 is to be read within the context of the design document, it is embedded in it. It does make some sense, but is not completely understandable without additional information.

18. Formocracy (2012)

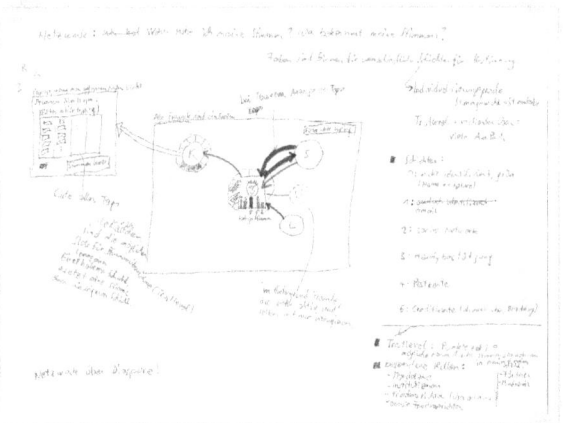

Figure 3. A first draft of the user interface system.

Hand drawn notations were not restricted to the development of high level game logic. Figure 3 shows a pen on paper draft for an aspect of the user-interface in *formocracy* (the user-profile page) plus some logic and explanatory comments. Making user-user and user-system intaraction possible, the interface must be as self explanatory as possible, while being capable of transferring all necessary actions and information. This makes the user-interface a notation system in its own right.

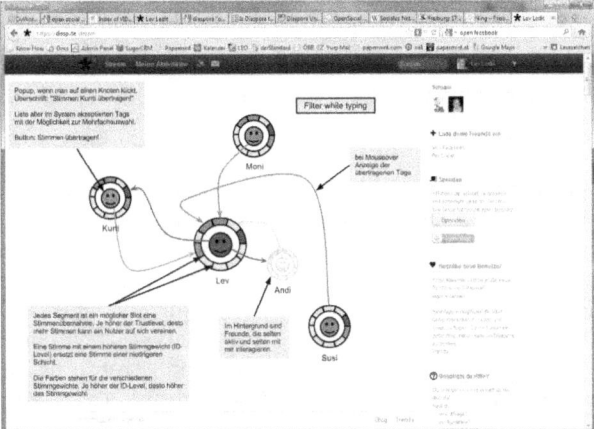

Figure 4. The user interface system in a more formal notation.

A mock-up of a user-profile page for *formocracy* is presented in Figure 4

A Few Specimens

with explanatory comments in boxes. Putting less of a demand on the abstraction capacities of the viewer, we produced the above mock-up for demonstration purposes only.

The development work is also, at this stage of realisation, still done with pen and paper.

Figure 5 shows a flowchart representation of out and ingoing information and user flow and loops of the *formocracy* platform with examples and minimal explanations done in textform for presentation purposes.

Especially when working on a project of such high complexity and with interdependencies between all kinds of aspects (from security-challenges to ethical standards to the fun factor), you learn very quickly that things have a very, very strong tendency to get more complex and complicated the more you work on them.

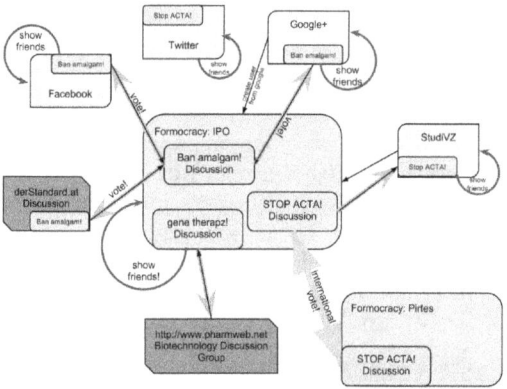

Figure 5. Describing the position of formocracy within a larger system of social and other media environments.

Initially we used mindmap-like representations to accompany our conversations, just to make sure we were talking about the same thing. Very soon these "maps" became our trusted method of navigation in the fast-growing landscape of thoughts that we created on our way. Unintentionally these original notations of our thoughts formed and influenced the way we structured and thought about their content. This feedback loop between our imagination of structures and their representation turned out to be extremely useful. In a way thinking about our own externalised thoughts created a creative system of "interactivity with self".

In our last transformational step all our notes, mindmaps, and flowcharts were collected and made publicly available in the form of a

18. Formocracy (2012)

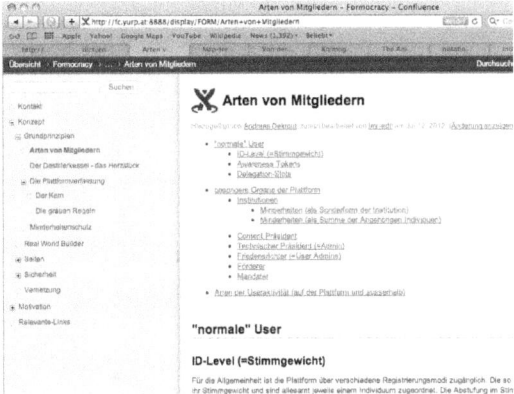

Figure 6. Design document for formocracy.

design document, as seen in Figure 6.[2]
While such a design document consists of structured text and explanatory and exemplary graphics, it must not be overseen that it is a "cooking-recipe" of its very own kind. When starting to actually program the software this is the one point of reference by which success or failure of the programmers is judged.

1. http://gamegestalt.com/
2. http://fc.yurp.at:8888/display/FORM/

A Few Specimens

WE TELL STORIES (2008)

Six To Start[1] is an Alternate Reality Game and Next Generation Narrative company based in London, UK. They create games, apps, and transmedia experiences for clients in the UK and overseas.

Mapping Reading - Navigating a Story Space

We Tell Stories was a collection of stories that Six To Start developed and presented in collaboration with the publishing house Penguin weekly for a period in 2008. The narratives were designed to use, in a non-trivial way, the possibilities of cross media narration. The opening story, "21 Steps," based upon *The 39 Steps*, plays out in a Google Maps environment. The rest of the stories use the online environment in different ways including blogs and Twitter. The last story, "The (former) General in his Labyrinth"[2] is a network of story elements that can be traversed by the reader as they move around in the General's labyrinth, the story dependent upon the reader's movements. It is described by Six To Start as "a rich and complex story by Mohsin Hamid, uses an entirely new form of branching storytelling to allow readers to explore the memories of an ageing, and not quite fictional, general."

The notation summarises the possible motions of the reader in the General's labyrinth. As the reader moves, certain story elements are played out. Passing back, the reader is confronted by an alternate history of the General's life. This path dependency makes the exploration of the General's world subjective in a simple yet non-trivial way

In his blog[3], Adrian Hon, who acted as the "Story architect" for the whole project and worked closely with all the people who implemented the story, said:

> Before Moshin began writing, I called him up to discuss the capabilities of our story architecture. I thought it was going to be a quick five minute call, but we ended up talking for about an hour, trying to work out what would be the most interesting – and achievable style of story. Ultimately Mohsin decided not to do a traditional branching narrative, and settled upon doing something else. Maybe a still life.
>
> Still life is a term I came up with earlier on, to describe one possibility in which readers could navigate around an essentially frozen world. There would be no branching narrative, but there would be branching paths, and readers would need and want to read all the cells. Imagine if you froze time, you could walk around and look through rooms in a building. Collectively those rooms

A Few Specimens

MAP OF STORY (Numbers [1] are cell text; arrows [->] are link direction; letters [AA] are link text; an asterisk [*] denotes a cell or link that changes during the story; and the ALICE reference is in Cell #5)

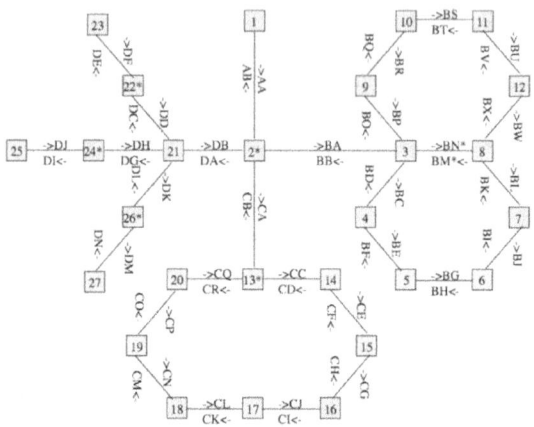

A flow chart of possible motion in the virtual palace, indicating which story elements are played out for the visitor depending upon their traversal of the joining edges.

would tell a single story, not a dozen different stories, and there would be no end.
[...]
I was genuinely impressed with the structure. To be honest, I think he understand the possibilities better than I do, because this is not a structure that I would have come up with myself. In a comparatively small number of cells, Mohsin managed to demonstrate three different styles of interactive storytelling, and link them together into a single overarching still life.
The (Former) General is not as visually impressive as some of the other stories, but I'm immensely proud of it. The interface, art design and story all meld together beautifully, and I believe it's the most innovative and original piece of storytelling in the six weeks. It's not quite a game, and while it does have branching, it doesn't allow the reader to affect the outcome of story, only their own experience of it.
It truly is something that you couldn't do in a book, and here, it tells a powerful tale as affecting as any novel.

The idea of a still life as a metaphor for an explorable story world is closely related to the example of *20 Seconds into the Future* above. In the palace, the movements between the elements convey story elements, which seem to be attached to the element but are actually path

19. We Tell Stories (2008)

dependent. In *20 Seconds into the Future*, the elements contain an overloading of information, which often only becomes clear as the memory of the elements is illuminated by a related story element in the space.

---

1. A startup investigating contemporary narratives.
   http://www.sixtostart.com/
2. *The (Former) General* online narrative:
   http://www.wetellstories.co.uk/stories/week6/ (accessed February 2013)
3. Hon's blog http://mssv.net/2008/04/22/creating-the-former-general/

A Few Specimens

GESTURAL NOTATION

Most of the examples of notation that we have seen and were investigating were written in some way. They might be coded or even dynamic, but they are largely archival. The use of gestures as a notation form counteracts this ideas of one of the functions of notation. In this chapter we will meet the *London Improvisors Orchestra* as well as the *Feral Choir* with some of their gestural notations.

Gestural realtime notation for an improvising orchestra

In improvising orchestras, the notation usually consists of live generated gestural hand signs. Some are repeatedly applied and used in multiple compositions, but some are created for very specific purposes. The set of symbols is introduced before a performance, and then the process of interaction between the conductor and the orchestra starts.

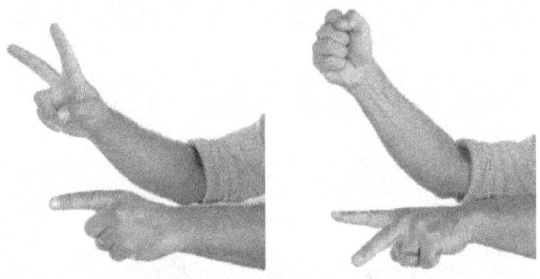

Two of the gestural notations used by the Improvisor's Orchestra

"One may ask why an Improvisers Orchestra has composers and/or conductors. The two free improvisations go to show that they do not actually need them. However, various people have come up with different ways to shape and direct the music, without using any conventional musical scores. Thus Dave Tucker's "conduction" is an example of the conductor determining who should be playing with what intensity at any given time. But he in turn is influenced by the feedback of what is actually played. Steve Beresford and Evan Parker work the same way, except that in both the examples heard here, one musician is free to play in a sort of concerto situation. Chris Burn achieves something similar, but uses a pre-determined sequence of who should be playing with whom to explore some of the myriad of small combinations that exist in

A Few Specimens

such an orchestra. Rhodri Davies investigates the potential quietness of a large ensemble, while Caroline Kraabel explores the organic processes of such a sensitive body. Simon H Fell's composition is perhaps the most controlled piece heard here, but even this leaves a considerable amount of freedom. Finally, there are two delightfully subversive attempts to produce random chance music - the antithesis of an improvising orchestra - by dividing the musicians into unrelating individuals (Adam Bohman) or independent sections (Philipp Wachsmann). All of the conductors and/or composers are members of the Orchestra, except for Dave Tucker who has performed with several of the musicians in other contexts as a guitarist." [1]

Phil Minton and the Feral Choir

In early October 2012, Phil Minton led a series of workshops with a group of trained and untrained singers. He has been doing this for many years and the choirs are known as the *Feral Choir* for each event. There was a performance on November 10th 2012 as part of the *Music Unlimited* festival in Wels, Austria. After the performance we interviewed two members of the choir as well as Phil Minton about the Feral Choir process.

The Feral Choir is a workshop structure to encourage people to use their voices. Phil Minton is well known for his work with highly non standard vocal techniques. *The Feral Choir* is a way into these techniques for participants, without the need for the self confidence and competence to enable a solo performance.

Minton leading the Feral Choir, showing some of the gestural notation he uses: Frozen Fragment, drunken football crowd, stop block and cut. (images Elisabeth Schedlberger)

In the performance, Minton acts as the conductor / composer. The choir is arranged in two rows of people, the full width of the stage. Minton moves along the choir using a collection of gestures to control the choir. Some of them are listed below, suffering the notational problems of conversion into written language.

- Parallel Hands: "Frozen Fragment." The hands indicate a section of the choir, a block, who each make a small sound fragment and then repeat it, looping, until instructed to stop.
- Parallel hands then crossing: The stop block command.
- Parallel hands with each hand circling: in this block, freely improvise.
- Thumbs Up: laughter.

20. Gestural Notation

- Thumbs down: "ohh" tone moving down, low pitched whinging, a feeling of dissapointment.
- Three fingers: Up makes W meaning "women" and down M meaning men, as a modifier for the next gesture.
- Two hands down, twiddling fingers: a muttering sound. Raising the hands (keeping fingers down) raises the volume and intensity until maximum is a drunken football crowd.
- Arms cuddling: "Lullaby" singing, quiet humming.
- Cut: spread fingers suddenly pulled into a downward fist to grab and stop a sound.

Minton also makes certain facial movements or even makes certain sounds to indicate the sort of sounds that a block should use. Shh, ZZZ sounds and facial expressions.

The gestures are principally clear analogues of the actions and effects that are being produced, with a low level of formalism. Some of the higher levels of formalism are culturally dependent (football crowd) and others such as the M and W are language dependent. He uses the same symbol set, slowly extending it, from one workshop or performance to the next. From a short interview with Minton after the performance he indicated that he uses no predefined score for the performance, using the gestural notation as a performative control method for improvisation.

1. Liner notes of *Proceedings* by the London Improvisers Orchestra, http://www.emanemdisc.com/E4201.html

A Few Specimens

ISORHYTHMIC VARIATIONS (2006)

Michael J. Schumacher[1] is a composer, performer and installation artist based in New York City. Schumacher works predominantly with electronic and digital media, specializing in computer generated sound environments that evolve continuously for long time periods.

> *ISORHYTHMIC VARIATIONS came about as an attempt to convert my installation "Noema" into a performance piece. Originally it was a commission from Ne(x)tworks Ensemble, who performed it at the Stone in NYC.*
> *Isorhythm is a technique used in the Middle Ages where a rhythmic pattern and melodic pattern of different lengths were repeated together. In this case, the rhythmic pattern is fixed, and is the same length for all players. Instead of a repeating melodic figure players choose from a group of motives, pitches, extended techniques, etc. Melodies emerge from the interaction of the ensemble.*

ISORHYTHMIC VARIATIONS may be performed with or without electronic "accompaniment".
A new version of ISORHYTHMIC VARIATIONS was composed in 2009 in collaboration with Sabrina Schroeder as part of an "exquisite corpse" composition.

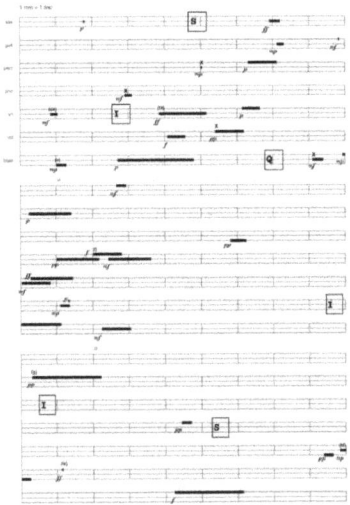

A Few Specimens

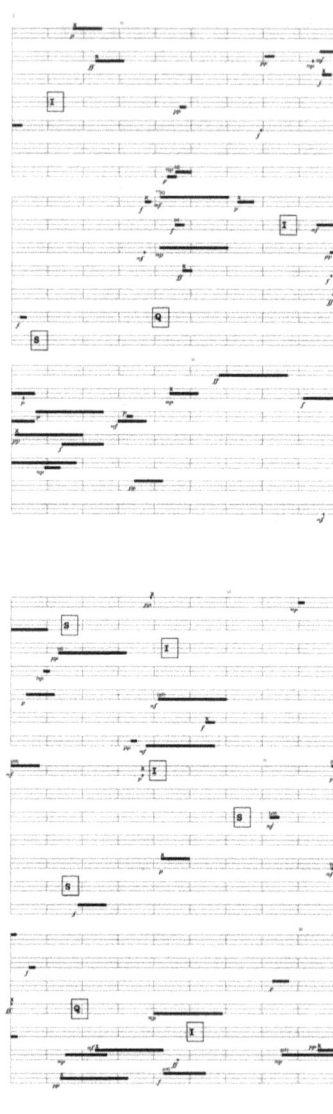

1. http://www.michaeljschumacher.com/

THE GREAT SCORE (2001 TO 2006)

A project[1] by Seppo Gründler and Elisabeth Schimana.
Elisabeth Schimana[2] was introduced in the *sitting in my chair* chapter.
Seppo Gründler[3] has been working with music, sound, communication, DIY media, software and electronic devices for 25 years, he is the director of the Masters program "Media and Interaction Design" at the University of Applied Sciences FH-Joanneum.
The basic idea for the composition and its performances is rooted in the historical context of electronic music. The concerts follow a precisely defined structure - the score. However the performing artists don't proceed according to a score in the traditional sense based on notes, but due to a temporal and functional structure. The work has been performed seven times by the composers and once by an extended group.
The material for *The Great Score* was worked on in seven cities. In each city, the material was created at that location and was presented, formed by the the base-structure, as an hour long concert. In the seventh performance all material resulted in a seven hour piece. In the eighth performance all interpretations resulted in a net-concert in their respective real locations and in virtual space.

Base Structure of the Score

The piece is in three movements.

Movement	1)	2)	3)
Gründler/ Schimana	material creation	freezing	regulation
Computer	data acquisition	analysis	synthesis
Visual	blocks with stripes	rings	red block

In each movement there is a role for the musicians, a role for the computer and a visual accompaniment to guide the performers.

First Movement

The first movement lasts for 28 minutes.
material creation 1)   Schimana transforms her voice with analogue

resonance filters and ring modulation. These will be controlled by a theremin antenna. Gründler uses his electric guitar as sound material and processes the sound with analogue and digital devices. The sounds created by one performer is meant as source material for the other, to be reworked at their discretion. The sound generators of each are crosswise connected with one another. The reciprocal access of material leads to a de-stabilization of each performer's control. Sounds coming from one person that are already dislodged from the event of their production. Discretionary power over the material changes from a dictatorial singular to a dialog. Especially noteworthy is the aesthetic of the performing practice, the live-context and the stage situation.

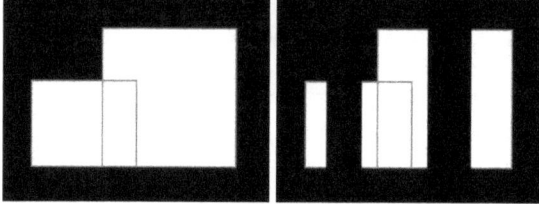

The first movement visuals. The initial shape grows black bars to indicate the passage of time, acting as a notational guide for the performers.

data acquisition 1) parallel to the creation of material, a computer records the audio data for later analysis. Independent from this, single loops will be generated.

1) Projections are generated as growing lines during the performance serving as the time structure for the performers. The performers could "feel" the light and therefore had orientation in time, instead of using a stop watch. At the time the black bars appear, the data acquisition starts.

 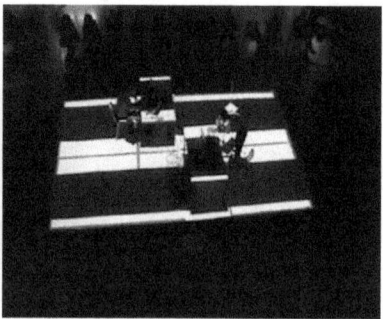

Performance at MAK, Vienna 2005. The growing bars (apparent in the second image) indicate time for the performers.

Second Movement

The second movement lasts for 21 minutes.
freezing 2) the short loops will be worked-over with analogue and digital processes and stacked as body of sound.
analysis 2) the structure and sound parameters for the following part (third movement) will be derived from the recorded audio data.
2) Ring by ring, the image is generated according to the total duration of the second part.

The pattern of red rings grows over the duration of the second movement, guiding the performers to the climax.

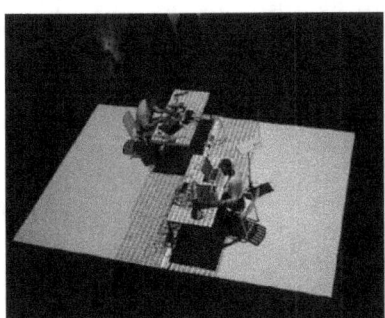 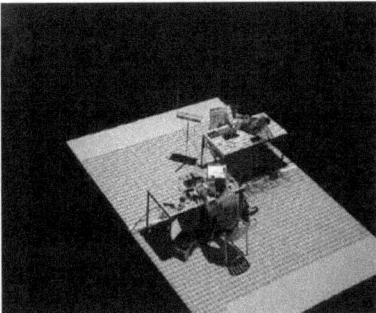

Performance at MAK, Vienna 2005, showing the growing pattern of red circles.

Third Movement

The third movement lasts for 7 minutes.
regulation 3) as sound directors, the performers subtly tamper with the generated sounds.
synthesis 3) based on the data from the analysis, the computer synthesizes the sound into a four-channel sound stream.

3) a static projection, generation is over. The image is a solid red block, flooding the stage completely.

Performance at MAK, Vienna 2005. The two projections are completely red, bathing the performers in a deep colour bath.

For the eighth performance, *networking*³, the score of the base-structure was left to artists in several locations for their interpretation. These interpretations resulted in performances in a net-concert at real locations and in virtual space on 1st of January 2006 as an ORF Kunstradio - Radiokunst[4] streaming concert.

1. http://partitur.at/
2. http://elise.at
3. http://gruendler.mur.at/
4. http://www.kunstradio.at/

20 SECONDS INTO THE FUTURE (2010)

Time's Up were introduced in the *Black Box Sessions* chapter.

Semantic Networks for Ideas

The Physical Narration installation *20 Seconds into the Future*[1] was shown at the "Long Night of Research" in November 2010 at the Johannes Kepler University in Linz, Austria. The piece is a room, apparently the room of a scientist, investigating the ways in which some mathematical ideas and some physical properties interact. The piece frames itself as a science and research communication piece. Visitors are welcomed into the room as if the scientist, Henry Kadigan, has just left and will be back shortly. They are asked to make themselves at home and look around the room. In the room there is not only the presentation of the work the character would have talked about, but it is also his working space.

As a result the visitor not only receives a presentation about science, but also about the life of a scientist, about the motivations to undertake science, to carry out experiments and research in general, to work the way he chose to. In the window a clock radio is playing a radio talkback show with the interviewee talking about their life as an independent scientist. Callers ask about non institutional science, raising issues with contemporary research practices, and a wide ranging conversation takes place. The radio show is formed in an endless loop, the listener always has the feeling to be in the middle of the show. Faxes arrive and messages are left on the answering machine about his life as an independent scientist, the lack of respect one receives and the freedom one has. In the corner the inactive machine that is seen in a video stands, in the video there is evidence presented of time travel into the future, where a watch undergoes the experience of travelling 20 seconds into the future. The sound effects match those from the next room - the visitor is lead to believe that Kadigan is in the next room and is currently travelling into the future - at least he will have the experience of spending a few minutes in the machine, while a much longer time will have passed. Feasible time travel is a lot more boring than the classical causal loop stuff of science fiction.

A Few Specimens

Visitors exploring the staged office of a fictional scientist.

The experience of visiting the space is one of following links from one object to another. A visitor finds something to be interested in, whether it be video, an interactive visualisation, a computer game, a mathematical genealogical tree or any number of other artefacts of the scientist's life. Listening to the radio show, the speakers chat about subjects that appear elsewhere in the room. The fax messages and answering machine offer suggestions, a letter next to the computer screen from a friend in Namibia adds some colour that explains a photo perched on the shelving and an artefact on the window sill. The form of the room is a network of objects, semantically linked by reference and similarity.

Thus for an analysis of the piece, we wanted to look at the way that various objects were semantically related. We collected many of the objects and joined them. The automatic graph visualisation package GraphViz was used to lay out the graph.

The resulting graph, which is by no means a complete mapping of all the objects in the space, shows the way that a visitor can move from a given object in the room to an idea, story element or concept and then onto other objects. From the fragment shown above, one can see that many of the concepts are related and reachable from some of the easily played with items such as the 3 sided Hyperbolic Pong game.

One element that is not attached to anything else, however, is the

23. 20 Seconds into the Future (2010)

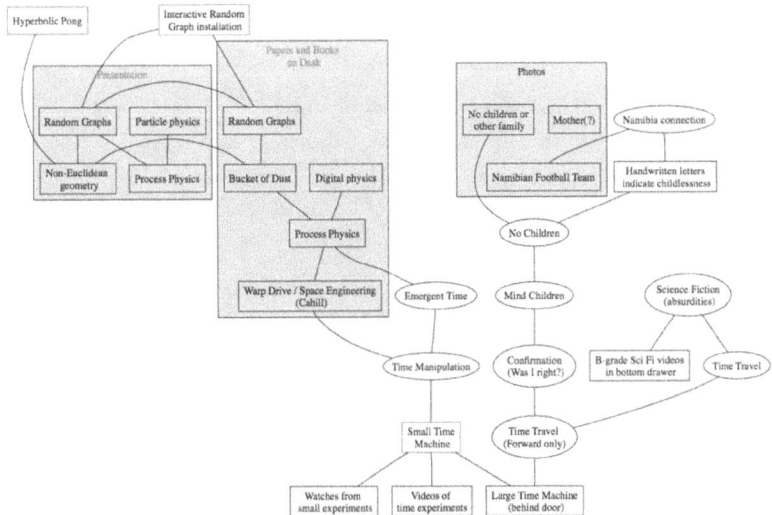

A section of a semantic net representation of objects in the office.

photograph of a woman who could be his mother. There is no indication on the back or elsewhere who this person might be, so the visitor is left to use their intuition based upon the clothing and hair style, the tint of the photo and its position in the room. However this photo is not connected to any other objects in the room, and only vaguely connected to the fact of his childlessness (this connection is only vague so has not been indicated in the diagram). Thus we could say that the photo is removable - we will not lose anything of importance by omitting it and may help clarify the installation by removing narrational clutter. Or it suggests that the story element needs to be better integrated, with a telephone call mentioning her or a letter from her tucked into the back of the photo frame.

This notational effort was of value in order to analyse the piece. A more comprehensive piece of notation would enhance the ability to evaluate the usefulness of each element of the installation. The purpose when creating these networks was similar, to see whether the visitor was passed on from element to element. This was not clear from the fragment, as it would only work when completed, so that all installation elements were present and could be looked at.

The notation would also help work out what smaller version of the piece could be presented in a way that would still work effectively. A reduced version should not have any isolated elements, for instance, as these indicate objects or situations in the space that are not conencting to anything else.

1. http://timesup.org/content/20-seconds-future

Some Words to Finish With

REFERENCES

We think it only fair to share with you some of the points of reference that we used as we constructed this book. Some of the references are very explicit, other references have been more pervasive. This list is by no means exhaustive.

Deleuze and Guattari 1987, *A Thousand Plateaus: Capitalism and Schizophrenia*. (B. Massumi, trans.) University of Minnesota Press.
Forsythe, W. 2009, *Choreographic Objects*. Essay released as part of a symposium, http://synchronousobjects.osu.edu/media (accessed February 2013).
Gansterer, N. 2011, *Drawing a Hypothesis*. Springer, Wien and New York.
Gethmann, D. 2010, *Klangmaschinen zwischen Experiment und Medientechnik*. Transcript Verlag.
Hawking, S., 1988, *A Brief History of Time*. Bantam Press.
Hofstadter, D., 1979, *Gödel, Escher, Bach: an Eternal Golden Braid*. Basic Books.
Holmgren, D. 2002, *Permaculture: Principles and Pathways beyond Sustainability*. Holmgren Design Services.
Korf, R., 1997, *Finding Optimal Solutions to Rubik's Cube Using Pattern Databases*. National Conference on Artificial Intelligence - AAAI 1997: pp 700-705.
Linde, C. & Labov, W., 1975, *Spatial Networks as a Site for the Study of Language and Thought*. Language 51:924-939.
Monmonier, M., 1996, *How to Lie with Maps*. University of Chicago Press.
Raymond, E. 1999, *The Cathedral and the Bazaar: Musings on Linux and Open Source by an Accidental Revolutionary*. O'Reilly Media.
Sauer, Th. 2009, *Notations 21*. Mark Batty Publisher.
Schmidt-Burkhardt A. 2003, *Maciunas' Learning Machines: From Art History to a Chronology of Fluxus*. Vice Versa Verlag.
Singmaster, D. 1981, *Notes on Rubik's 'Magic Cube.'* Enslow Pub Inc.
Solomon, M. R. and H. Assael, 1987, *The Forest or the Trees: A Gestalt Approach to Symbolic Consumption*. In Donna Jean Umiker-Sebeok, ed., *Marketing and Semiotics: New directions in the study of signs for sale*. New York: Mouton de Gruyter. P. 189-216.
Williams, Raymond, 1973, *The Country and the City*. New York: Oxford University Press.

Some Words to Finish With

A CLOSING CAKE

We have reached the end of this sprint and the end of this book. This chapter wishes to thank you by sharing the abstraction of a delicious cake that Lisa, our wonderful cook, shared with us.
But first we will attempt to notate the history and process of this book.

History

This book is designed to be extended. It is to a large degree a selfish book - most of the people writing are looking at ways that notational techniques can help them better explain, explore and discuss their own work. Thus the book is very explicitly open and we are looking forward to further versions taking the ideas a lot further forward so we can learn from the later writers. Feel free, feel welcome, to contribute and make this book as much yours as you would like to.

Version 1.2

The printed version was heavily proof read by Elisabeth Schimana and Pippa Buchanan and the corrections included. The Gestural Notation chapter was expanded and many small changes were made. Image placement was improved. The latest version took in the newest developments in BookJS (version 0.70dev) and Booktype (version 1.6) in order to massage itself into existence. This version will be offered as a book and epub. Feel free to join in and help create the next versions at http://marta.booktype.pro/turtles-and-dragons where we encourage participation.

Version 1.1

Created in the month following the book sprint with the explicit desire to have a printed version. In this process the paper presented by Bob Rotenberg at Data Ecologies 2012 was developed into a chapter. Some examples were added and the density of connections between the chapters developed.
This version of the text will be offered as a printed book.

Some Words to Finish With

Version 1.0

This is version 1.0 of our point of view on Notation. We have slept little and written too much, discussed more and learnt a wide variety of things. This version can stand on its own feet, but it is also growing. Thus we would like to welcome you, the reader, to contribute to it. We see several things that would have a place in later versions:

- Bob Rotenburg's presentation paper at the Data Ecologies Symposium offers a far more intricately worked out set of thoughts about the contexts of notation that we have managed. We hope to develop a version that can grow in here as a new chapter.
- Examples of other works, from a variety of sources, would help round out techniques and ideas. We are a very finite group of people with a very specific set of experiences. So a broad range of new examples would help inform the further development of the book
- Several themes have been moved to the Hold chapter to be dealt with properly. Topics such as treating legal and other social contract systems as notational systems have been thrown around but we have agreed that they require more time and effort then we can give them in this context.

Version 1.0 was created between September 5 and 10, 2012, by Elisabeth Schimana, Andreas Dekrout, Simone Boria, Marta Peirano, Heather Kelley, Rachel O'Reilly, Tim Boykett and Adam Hyde in a book sprint at the Kunstraum Goethestrasse in Linz Austria. The sprint was part of the Physical and Alternate Reality Narratives (PARN) project with the support of the Culture Programme 2007 - 2013 of the European Union, the City of Linz, the State of Upper Austria and the Federal BMUKK. PARN is a project from Time's Up, FoAM, Blast Theory and Lighthouse investigating new forms of storytelling in physical and alternate reality spaces.

This Book Sprint was the second phase of an investigation that started at the Data Ecologies 2012 event with the subtitle "The Map and The Territory." Three of the participants, Simone Boria, Elisabeth Schimana and Tim Boykett were present at that event. The documentation[1] of the event, prepared by Emilie Giles and Monique Alvarez, had been made recently available and was of value, particularly to those who had not been present. These were Andreas Dekrout, Marta Pierano and Heather Kelley, who skimmed and scanned the documentation but did not get too deep within. We had been warned by our Book Sprint facilitator, Adam Hyde, to avoid having too many fixed points in the planned book, that the symposium documentation might be more of a hindrance than a help. The process of a Book Sprint is getting increasingly well defined but not well understood outside the mind of Adam, so the last person present, Rachel O'Reilly, was here to

25. A Closing Cake

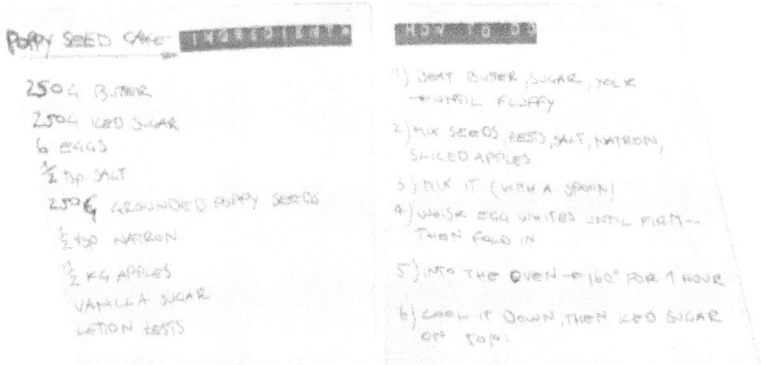

The recipe as supplied

document the process and observe the techniques used. We eagerly await her results, so as to better understand what was happening to us. Rachel also brought with her a critical eye and fast fingers to help get some of the wonderfully spoken but hard to write parts of the process down into the book. Last but not least, Johannes Grenzfurthner/monochrom jumped in with some cover art and we are ready to rock and roll.

Recipe

This Poppy Seed Cake arrived on the Thursday. Unfortunately we cannot pack a slice in a PDF or a book, so we send on the most practical of all notations, a recipe.

Poppy Seed Cake

Ingredients: 250g butter, 250g icing sugar, 6 eggs, 1/2 tsp. salt, 250g ground poppy seeds, 1/2 tsp. natron (=Baking Soda), 500g apples, vanilla sugar, lemon zest.
How to:
1) Beat butter, sugar, yolk until fluffy;
2) mix seeds, zests, salt, natron, sliced apples;
3) mix it (with a spoon);
4) whisk egg whites until firm - then fold in;
5) into the oven with 160° for 1 hour;
6) cool it down, then sprinkle some more icing sugar on top!

Some Words to Finish With

Sponsors

Disclaimer

"This project has been funded with support from the European Commission. This publication reflects the views only of the authors, and the Commission cannot be held responsible for any use which may be made of the information contained therein."

1. Wiki containing documentation:
   http://wiki.physicalnarration.org/wiki/index.php/DE12TheMapAndTheTerritory

www.ingramcontent.com/pod-product-compliance
Lightning Source LLC
Chambersburg PA
CBHW060853170526
45158CB00001B/339